Old Testament Portraits of Christ

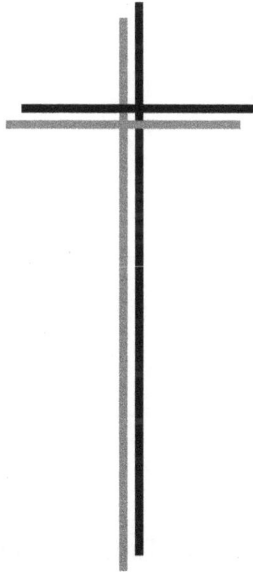

**Devotional Readings
to Refresh the Spirit
and Grow in Grace**

Dr. John W. Tape

All Scripture passages are taken from the Holy Bible, New International Version®. NIV®. Copyright 1973, 1978, 1984, by the International Bible Society. Used by permission of Zondervan Publishing House. All rights reserved.

ISBN: 978-0-6152-0656-1

Table of Contents

Old Testament Portraits of Christ

Introduction

The following devotions are based upon a biblical method of interpretation that uses several main principles. The first principle is to respect the historical understanding of the text. This perspective emphasizes that the Bible is grounded in history in such a way that the events it portrays are historically true and reliable (Luke 1:1-4, John 15:26-27, Acts 1:21-22, Heb. 2:3-4, 2 Pet. 1:16, 1 John 1:1). Fictitious stories in the Bible, such as the parables, are clearly distinct from its historical narratives. The Bible is to be taken at face value. It means what it says. To find the correct understanding of a text, the reader need not search behind the text to discover some unwritten "real" message of the authors. Nor is it necessary to decipher a text using some secret code. God loves us far too much to make understanding His word so esoteric and mysterious. Luther explains, "It is the historical sense alone which supplies the true and sound doctrine." [1]

The second principle used is to recognize the Christo-centric understanding of the Bible. The reader must ask of each text—Old and New Testament alike—"What does this passage tell me about Christ?" For Christ is the heart and core of the entire Bible. Jesus explained this to the two disciples on the road to Emmaus (Luke 24:27)

---

[1] Luther's Works, 55 vols. , eds, J. Pelikan and H. T. Lehmann, American Edition in English Translation (Philadelphia: Fortress Press and St. Louis: Concordia Publishing House, 1958-1986), 1:233. Hereafter, this work is abbreviated as L.W.

and again to the rest of the disciples (Luke 24:44-45). Luther writes,

> God is particularly concerned about our knowledge of the revelation of His Son, as seen throughout the Old and the New Testament. All points to the Son. . . . Thus all of Scripture . . . is pure Christ, God's and Mary's Son. Everything is focused on this Son, so that we might know Him distinctively . . . To him who has the Son Scripture is an open book; and the stronger his faith in Christ becomes, the more brightly will the light of Scripture shine for him.[2]

Again Luther says, "All the stories of Holy Writ, if viewed aright, point to Christ."[3]

There is a third principle used in some of these devotions. That is the allegorical (or symbolic) method of interpretation. This method, which has its roots in the Bible itself, was used in the early church (especially in Alexandria) and became very popular during the Middle Ages. However, it eventually fell into disrepute—for good reason. It was horribly misused. Many theologians would allegorize a passage by tearing it from its historical context and reading into it a symbolic meaning that was completely foreign to the intended meaning of the original author. In this way, Scripture became a wax sculpture, which could be twisted and shaped to suit anyone's latest whim. During the Reformation, this custom of allegorizing scripture was relegated to the dustbin of history. Many would say "Good riddance!"

---

[2] L.W. 15:338-339.
[3] L.W. 22:339.

Yet, perhaps we should not be so hasty. Couldn't there be a proper use for allegory? Just because it was misused does not mean that it cannot be properly used. St. Paul used this method in Gal. 4:21-5:6 where Hagar and Sarah represent the two covenants. He also allegorizes in Eph. 5:25-32 where he says marriage symbolizes the relationship between Christ and the church, and again in Rom. 5:14 where he states that Adam represents Christ.[4] St. Peter allegorizes in 1 Pet. 3:21 where he writes that the water of the Noachian flood represents Baptism. These examples would indicate that not all allegorizing needs to be abandoned. But to the contrary, both Peter and Paul, writing under the inspiration of the Holy Spirit, have shown us a model that we would do well to follow.

Luther explains the proper use of allegories when he writes, "After this [*i.e., the historical sense*], has been treated and correctly understood then one may also employ allegories as an adornment and flowers to embellish or illuminate the account."[5]

Once the reader understands the true historical sense of the passage, then an allegory can be used to explain, illustrate, or apply biblical truth. Luther opines,

> But after the foundation has been laid by other unerring and clear passages of Scripture, what should keep one from introducing an allegory not only to embellish but also to teach the subject more clearly? . . . Therefore, Augustine correctly says that a figure proves nothing and should have no place in a dispute. For it is necessary to lay a

---

[4] L.W. 1:233-234.
[5] L.W. 1:233.

firm foundation in a dispute. After this has been done, there is nothing to keep one from making the subject clearer and embellishing it with an allegory or a figure." [6]

Again Luther explains in more detail,

> Origen, Jerome, Augustine, and Bernard allegorize a great deal. The trouble is that since they spend too much time on allegories, they call hearts away and make them flee from the historical account and from faith, whereas allegories should be so treated and designed that faith, to which the historical accounts point in every instance, may be aroused, increased, enlightened, and strengthened . . . I urge you with all possible earnestness to be careful to pay attention to the historical accounts. But wherever you want to make use of allegories, do this: follow closely the analogy of the faith, that is, adapt them to Christ, the church, faith, and the ministry of the Word. [7]

Thus, Luther follows the example of the New Testament writers. He stresses the importance of the historical understanding of Scripture; but still allows for allegories when they are used correctly—when they illustrate the Scripture, encourage our faith, and direct us to Christ.

Some of these devotions try to resurrect this long-forgotten method of allegorizing in the hope of drawing

---

[6] *D. Martin Luthers Werke, Kritisch Gesamtausgabe*, 64 Bände (Weimar, 1883—) 43:12. This English translation is taken from Ewald Plass, ed., *What Luther Says* (St. Louis: Concordia Publishing House, 1959), 1:100 #308.
[7] L.W. 2:164.

attention to Christ and the eternal salvation He earned for us. The reader may determine if the attempt has been successful.

This book is intended for personal private reading. However, it also may be used beneficially for family and classroom devotions, as well as small group Bible studies. It may be used to strengthen Christians in their faith and to show non Christians what they are missing. Pastors looking for sermon ideas and illustrations will find this a storehouse full of treasures that sparkle with the light of the Gospel.

Finally, I must give credit to whom credit is due. Some of the ideas in this book are not original with me, but come from Johann Gerhard.[8] Like Luther before him, Gerhard emphasized the historical understanding of the Bible and clearly understood Christ as the heart and center of all Scripture. He also employed the proper use of allegories. In some of these devotions, I have merely mined the nuggets of gold produced by this brilliant 17th century theologian and expanded them for the benefit of 21st-century readers. May our gracious Lord grant to His church more minds like that of Gerhard, and may He use these devotions to draw you, the reader, closer to Himself.

–Dr. John W. Tape

---

[8] Johann Gerhard, *Postilla,* trans. Rev. Dr. Elmer M. Hohle (Malone, Texas: The Center for the Study of Lutheran Orthodoxy, 2001).

For everything that was written in the past was written to teach us, so that through endurance and the encouragement of the Scriptures we might have hope.

Romans 15:4

Creator of Adam
Giver of Life

Readings: Genesis 2:7 and John 20:19-22

On the sixth day of creation, the Lord took clay from the ground and shaped it into the form of a man. Initially this shape was lifeless. Its eyes did not see. Its heart did not beat. Its brain did not reason. This clay figure could not walk or talk. Nor could it laugh or love. It could not appreciate the azure blue sky or the scent of the crocus. Nor could it taste the sweetness of an orange or feel the soft grass on which it lay. It lay on the ground cold, lifeless, and loveless. But in an instant all that changed.

The Lord "breathed into his nostrils the breath of life and the man became a living being" (Gen. 2:7). That instant his eyes were opened. He looked into the face of his Creator and his heart filled to overflowing with joy for life and love for his Lord. In that second Adam became a child of God. Now his body, which was formerly lifeless, had life eternal. He, who was powerless, received strength from God (Ps. 18:1; 2 Sam. 22:33). He, who had no spirit, became the temple of the Holy Spirit (1 Cor. 6:19).

What a difference the breath of God makes when that breath bestows His Holy Spirit! It is the difference between life and death (Ezek. 37:1 -14). This is what Jesus does. He breathes on His people His life-giving Holy Spirit. On the evening of the first Easter, the grief-stricken disciples were hiding behind locked doors. Mary Magdalene and the other women tried to tell them Jesus had risen, but the disciples refused to believe them (Luke 24:10-11). Filled with fear and grief, the disciples were not all that different from the original figure of clay shaped by God in the Garden of Eden. They could not appreciate the beauty of nature. They could not go into the world and share God's love with others. Their strength, their energy, their zeal for life was gone. In many respects they had no life—no real life with Christ. Then in an instant all that changed. Jesus appeared and breathed on them, and they received the Holy Spirit.

The disciples received new life, by the Holy Spirit, who was given to them by Jesus' breath (John 20:19-22). Their lives were renewed, rejuvenated—reborn. They could now grow in their faith toward God and in their love for one another. They could go out into Jerusalem, Judea, Samaria, and to the ends of the earth to share the message of God's love.

Like the disciples and Adam before them, this is what Jesus also does for you. Without Jesus, you would have no life—no real life with Christ. But He has breathed into us His Holy Spirit so we are born anew (John 3:3- 10, 16). Now because of Jesus we live with renewed strength, vigor, and vitality. In this new life He gives, all things work together for us (Rom. 8:28). In this new life, God is for us (Rom. 8:31). In this new life, we will live forever with Him who died and rose again for us.

Prayer: Heavenly Father, I thank You that You have given me the gift of life. But even more, I am thankful that You sent Jesus into the world so he could breathe into my life Your Holy Spirit that I might be born anew and live with You forever. Amen.

Eve
Suitable Helper

Readings: Genesis 2:19-24 and Luke 7:11-17

After God created all the animals, He placed Adam in the Garden of Eden. It became Adam's responsibility to give the animals names. God brought the animals to Adam, "to see what he would name them; and whatever the man called each living creature, that was its name. So the man gave names to all the livestock, the birds of the air and the beasts of the field" (Gen. 2:19). Adam must have marveled at the beauty, splendor, and diversity of God's animal kingdom. Yet, as wonderful as these creatures were, "no suitable helper was found" (Gen. 2:20).

Did Adam think he would find a suitable helper from among the animals? As he gave the animals their names was he looking for the right one to be his companion in life? If so, he was very disappointed. Even after surveying all the animals, Adam was still very alone and that was not good (Gen. 2:18). Only when Adam finished naming all the animals did God then create Eve. It is as though God were saying, "Adam, don't be disappointed. You haven't seen anything yet. Wait till you see the special companion I will make specifically for you. In her, you will have a suitable, lifelong partner—one better than you ever imagined."

When Adam first saw Eve, he knew she was the one. From God's entire creation, Eve was the only one with which Adam could truly share his life. Only with Eve could he share a future, a love, and a family. Only she could be a suitable helper. This directs our attention to the ultimate suitable helper—the Lord Himself.

All of us need help in life. We need help to be strong when we are weak. We need help being patient when we are angry. We need help forgiving when we are vengeful. We need help to do the right thing when we are tempted.

From where does our help for such things come? If we are like Adam and look in the wrong place, we like Adam will be disappointed. Isaiah asked the people of Jerusalem, "To whom will you run for help?" (Is 10:3). Many of the people in his day were looking for help in the wrong place (Is. 30:1-3; 31:1). They were going to be greatly disappointed (Is. 57:13). Suitable help could only be found in the Lord (Is. 41:10-14).

The psalmist also knew God was his only help when he wrote, "I lift up my eyes to the hills—where does my help come from? My help comes from the Lord, the Maker of heaven and earth" (Ps.121:1-2). So also we look to the hills for our help, specifically to Mount Calvary. In Jesus "God has come to help His people" (Luke 7:16). In Him alone we find our ultimate suitable helper. Only in Him do we find our help for confronting life's every challenge.

Prayer: Lord Jesus, I cry to You for help. Come to the aid of all who call upon Your name. Uphold the weak with the power of Your righteous right hand. Let all who need help find their ultimate help in You. Amen.

Abel
Innocent Victim

Readings: Genesis 4:1-12 and 1 Peter 1:18-19

After Adam and Eve were expelled from the Garden of Eden they had two sons, Cain and Abel. Abel was a shepherd and Cain was a farmer (Gen. 4:2). They both sacrificed their offerings to God. God accepted Abel's offering. But he did not accept Cain's. Heb.11:4 tells us, "Abel offered God a better sacrifice than Cain did."

We do not know what made Cain's offering inferior. Perhaps he did not sacrifice to God the best of his crops. Or maybe his heart was not right, and he offered his sacrifice reluctantly. In any case, God accepted the offering of Abel but not that of Cain. Cain could have repented, but instead his heart was filled with a jealous rage. God warned him (Gen. 4:6-7). But Cain did not heed God's Word.

In a fit of jealous rage, Cain "attacked his brother and killed him" (Gen. 4:8). Abel did not deserve to die. He did nothing wrong. Yet, he was the victim who suffered at the hands of a sinful man. Innocent blood was shed. Later, the Lord came to Cain and said, "What have you done? Listen! Your brother's blood cries out to Me from the ground" (Gen. 4:10).

So it is with Jesus. He was as innocent as Abel. Jesus had done nothing wrong. He was guilty of no crime. He was completely without sin (1 Pet. 2:22). Yet, his innocent blood was shed on the cross. By whom? By His brothers!

You and I—we are His brothers and sisters in our humanity. His death is our fault. It is not the Father's fault, although He sent Jesus into the world to die (Is. 53: 6-7). It is not Satan's fault even though he convinced Judas to betray Him (Luke 22:3). It is the fault of sinful humanity. Our sins nailed Jesus to the cross. Our sins made His innocent death necessary (1 Pet. 2:24). We are as guilty of Jesus' death as Cain was of Abel's.

Yet there is a vital difference. Abel's blood cried out for vengeance. Abel's blood caused Cain to be cursed (Gen. 4:10-11); whereas, the blood of Jesus, "speaks a better word than the blood of Abel" (Heb. 12:24). The blood of Jesus causes us to be blessed. The blood of Jesus "purifies us from all sin" (1 John 1:7), and reconciles us to God (Col. 1:19-20). Jesus died on the cross and shed His innocent blood for you.

Glory be to Jesus, Who in bitter pains
Poured for me the life-blood from His sacred veins.
Grace and life eternal in that blood I find;
Blest be His compassion, infinitely kind.
Abel's blood for vengeance pleaded to the skies
But the blood of Jesus for our pardon cries.
(*Glory Be to Jesus,* stanza 1, 2, 4)

Prayer: Dear Jesus, I thank You that You did not hold my sins against me. But You loved me so much You were willing to go to the cross and have Your innocent blood shed for me so that I could have the forgiveness of all my sins and be reconciled to our heavenly Father. Help me to trust in your work always. Amen.

Noah
Savior

Readings: Genesis 6:9-22 and 1 Peter 3:18-21

What fool would build such a big boat? Oh, how the people must have ridiculed him. For the times of Noah were evil. "Every inclination of the thoughts of his [man's] heart was only evil all the time" (Gen. 6:5). It is possible Noah tried to warn them. Can't you see him wiping the sweat from his brow and setting aside his saw long enough to plead with the nearby mockers? Just as Ezekiel would later say to Israel, "Repent! Turn away from all your offenses; then sin will not be your downfall. Rid yourselves of all the offenses you have committed, and get a new heart and a new spirit" (Ezek. 18:30-31). Perhaps the Lord would show mercy. He takes no pleasure in the death of anyone (Ezek. 18:32).

Didn't Jesus also warn the people of their destruction? Even as He was being led to crucifixion, he told the women of their impending doom (Luke 23:28-31). Still like the people of Noah's time, many ridiculed (Luke 23:35-37).

But in spite of the derision, Noah and Jesus continued their work. Noah built the ark, not only for the animals, but also to prepare salvation for those few people who heeded God's Word. Noah, his wife, their three sons and their wives—eight in all were saved from drowning (Gen. 7:13). Carrying the ark, the floodwaters lifted Noah and his family above the devastation. So also Jesus, on the wooden cross prepared eternal salvation for all people.

Be-cause of His work, the water of our baptism now lifts us up and saves us from the devastation of everlasting condemnation (1 Pet. 3: 21-22).

At the time of Noah, everything perished (Gen. 6:17); likewise, at the end of the world, the earth as we know it will be destroyed (2 Pet. 3:10). Yet, those who believe and trust in the Lord will be saved, because He has prepared the ark of our salvation through His death on the cross.

After the flood, the curse was removed (Gen. 8:21). God gave us the rainbow as His unending promise that He would never flood the world again (Gen. 9:12 17). Likewise, Jesus removed from us the curse—the curse that we rightfully deserve because of our sin.

Now, because of Jesus, God will only give us His love. That is His promise to you. As God told Isaiah long ago, "This is like the days of Noah, when I swore that the waters of Noah would never again cover the earth. So now I have sworn not to be angry with you, never to rebuke you again. Though the mountains be shaken and the hills be removed, yet My unfailing love for you will not be shaken nor My covenant of peace be removed" (Is. 54:9-10). Let the rainbow serve as a reminder that in Jesus we will never experience God's wrath—because He has prepared our salvation.

Prayer: Heavenly Father, I thank You for Noah. Through him You saved one family from the flood. But I give You even greater thanks for Jesus, through whom You have accomplished eternal salvation for all people. Amen.

Melchizedek
A Different Priest

Readings: Genesis 14: 17-20 and Hebrews 7: 11-25

Of all the people in the Bible, Melchizedek is one of the most mysterious. We know nothing about his family, his birth, his death, or how he became a priest. As Heb. 7:3 says, Melchizedek is "without father or mother, without genealogy, without beginning of days, or end of life, like the Son of God." Like the Son of God indeed.

Jesus too was mysterious. Many people thought they knew Jesus, but they didn't. Some thought He was the son of Joseph (Luke 3:23; 4:22). But He was not (Matt. 1:18-21). Some thought they knew His family. But they did not know His true brothers and sisters (Matt. 12:46-50).

Some thought they knew where He came from (Luke 23:6-7), but they did not know His true origins (John 3:13; 8:56-58). Like Melchizedek, for many people, Jesus was shrouded in mystery. But there is even a greater similarity.

Referring to the coming Messiah, King David wrote, "You are a priest forever, in the order of Melchizedek" (Ps. 110:4). Melchizedek and Jesus were priests, but they were not like all the others. All other priests were members of the tribe of Levi and descendents of Aaron (Num. 3:10).

Whereas, Melchizedek lived long before Aaron, and Jesus was of the tribe of Judah. Neither one were Levitical priests. They were definitely of a different order. The Levitical priests offered sacrifices on behalf of themselves, as well as the other people (Lev. 9:7).

It was also necessary for them to repeat their sacrifice for the sins of the people every day (Ex. 29:36-37). When Jesus offered up His body as the sacrifice for our sins on the altar of the cross, He did not have to suffer for His own sins, nor did He ever have to repeat it. His sacrifice was once and for all (Heb. 7:26-27).

The Levitical priests could only serve temporarily. They all eventually died. However, the priesthood of Jesus lasts forever. He is always there to intercede for you before the throne of His heavenly Father (Heb. 7:23-25). Jesus was certainly a different priest, as was Melchizedek.

The name Melchizedek means "King of Righteousness" or "King of Peace" (Heb. 7:2). This name also describes Jesus. He is the "Prince of Peace" (Is. 9:6). He is "The Lord Our Righteousness" (Jer. 23:5-6). In Jesus, we are given true peace and righteousness. His priesthood guarantees that forever.

Prayer: Heavenly Father, I thank You that Jesus is a different kind of priest. Rather than sacrificing bulls or lambs, He gave up Himself on the altar of the cross. I thank You that His priesthood will last forever, and He will always intercede on my behalf. Help me to trust in Him always. Amen.

Jacob's Ladder
Mediator

Readings: Genesis 28: 10-17 and 1 Timothy 2:5

Jacob was a scoundrel. In ancient Israel, his name became proverbially associated with deception (Hos. 12:2). He cheated his brother (Gen. 25:29-34), and lied to his father (Gen. 27:1-40). His brother Esau hated him so much he planned to kill Jacob (Gen. 27: 41). Their mother, fearing that her two sons might kill each other, sent Jacob away to live with her brother Laban in Haran (Gen. 27:42-45).

One night on his way to Haran, Jacob had the most peculiar dream. In his dream, he saw a stairway reaching from earth to heaven—with angels ascending and descending on it. There the Lord appeared to him and promised, "I am with you and will watch over you wherever you go . . . I will not leave you" (Gen. 28:15). In spite of all the deceiving he had done, the Lord still loved him. Jacob was so moved by this when he awoke he said, "How awesome is this place! This is none other than the house of God; this is the gate of heaven" (Gen. 28:17). So he called the place "Bethel" (which means house of God).

This stairway reminds us of Jesus. He is the stairway between earth and heaven (John 1:51). It is through Jesus that God descends from heaven to earth (Matt. 1:22-23; John 3:31). It is through Jesus that we ascend from earth to heaven (Matt. 25:34).

First, God descends to us making possible our ascent to Him. Jesus makes this happen. He is the only mediator between God and man (1 Tim. 2:5). There is no other way to heaven but through Jesus. He alone is the gate to heaven (John 10:7). As He said, "I am the way no man comes to the Father but by me" (John 14:6).

The responsibility of a mediator is to bridge the gulf that separates two parties. The mediator does not just represent one party (Gal. 3:20). Rather, he represents both parties to each other to heal the wounds, resolve the disagreements and bring reconciliation.

Jesus does this. He presents the Father to us as one full of grace, mercy and forgiveness (Luke 15:11-31)—one whose steadfast love endures forever (Ps. 136). To the Father in heaven, Jesus presents us holy, pure, and blameless (Col. 1:21-22). Only Christ, the one who is both God and man in Himself, can bridge the gulf between God and man.

This is so unlike the Tower of Babel where the people said, "Come let us build ourselves a city, with a tower that reaches to the heavens" (Gen. 11:4). They wanted to reach heaven by their own works. But their grandiose endeavor failed miserably. So it is still today. All attempts for us to reach heaven apart from Christ are doomed to fail. Christ is the only bridge that can span the distance between earth and heaven—between you and your loving heavenly Father.

Prayer: Heavenly Father, because of my sin there would be a huge chasm between us. It would be a separation I could never cross. But in Your mercy, You sent Your only Son to bridge that distance. Thank you. Amen.

Reuben
Sees Our Misery

Readings: Genesis 29:31-32 and Luke 1:26-31

Leah was not happy. Jacob had two wives and Rachel was his favorite. Leah was number two—the second fiddle. Although she was the first to marry Jacob, she was not first in his heart (Gen. 29:30).

The Bible does not tell us how Jacob expressed his favoritism. Perhaps it was something blatant and obvious—like the coat of many colors he would later give his favorite son (Gen. 37:3). Or perhaps it was subtler, like the look in his eyes or the tone of his voice— something that only Leah could notice. Either way, her second rate status made her miserable. But one day something miraculous happened.

"When the Lord saw that Leah was not loved, he opened her womb . . . Leah became pregnant and gave birth to a son. She named him Reuben, for she said, 'It is because the Lord has seen my misery' " (Gen. 29:31-32). That name was very appropriate. In Hebrew, the name "Reuben" sounds very similar to the Hebrew for "he has seen my misery."

Years later, Reuben would behold the misery of his little brother Joseph. When his brothers were filled with jealously, they sought to kill Joseph. But Reuben stepped in to save him. "So Joseph went after his brothers and found them near Dothan. But they saw him in the distance, and before he reached them, they plotted to kill him. 'Here comes that dreamer!' they said to each other. 'Come now, let us kill him and throw him into one of these cisterns and say that a ferocious animal devoured him' . . . When Reuben heard this, he tried to rescue him from their hands. 'Let's not take his life,' he said, 'Don't shed any blood. Throw him into this cistern here in the desert, but don't lay a hand on him.' Reuben said this to rescue him from them and to take him back to his father" (Gen. 37:17-22).

Reuben, the firstborn of Jacob and Leah, was the oldest of the brothers. By speaking up and putting a stop to their murderous plans, he saved Joseph from certain death. Surely it was because Reuben saw the misery of Joseph that he took pity on him and saved him. Yet, the name "Reuben" in Hebrew means, "behold, a son." Reuben was the firstborn son of Jacob.

But his act of saving Joseph points to a greater son—Mary's firstborn, who saw our misery—and in His great pity came into the world to rescue us. Yes, there is misery in this world. There may be misery in your life brought about by yourself or by others. But as with Leah, and Joseph, the Lord has seen your misery. He has heard your cry (Ex. 23:25). He came into the world as a son—the firstborn of Mary, to rescue and comfort us in our darkest hours.

Prayer: Dear Jesus, I thank You that even before I was born You knew me. You knew what challenges, difficulties, and miseries I would have in my life. In Your great mercy, You came into the world as the firstborn son born of Mary to rescue me. Thank You. Amen.

Joseph
Merciful

Readings: Genesis 50:15-21 and 1 John 1:9

Joseph had every right to be furious—not only for what his brothers did to him, but also for what they did to their father. His brothers sold him into slavery for a few pieces of silver (Gen. 37:28). Then to make things even worse, they broke their father's heart, when they lied to him saying that a wild beast killed his youngest son (Gen. 37:31-35).

Many years later Joseph was in position for revenge. He had become the second most powerful person in all Egypt (Gen. 41:40). He could have them all thrown into prison or even executed. Their lives were in his hands. They were terrified and rightfully so.

So also, Christ could throw us into everlasting punishment. We have wronged Him and His Father. We have not loved Him with our whole heart. Our faith is weak and inconsistent. Our love for others is marred by selfishness. We have every right to be terrified of God and of His just retribution. We deserve only His wrath and punishment (Eph. 2:1-3).

Yet, what did Joseph do to his brothers? He did not punish them as they deserved. He showed mercy rather than revenge. Moved to tears by his love and compassion, he forgave their sins, told them they had no need to fear, and assured them of his future care (Gen. 50:17-21). Here we have a beautiful picture of the mercy that is ours in Jesus Christ.

Like Joseph, Jesus also was handed over for a few pieces of silver (Matt. 26:15). Like Joseph, Jesus is also in a position of authority (Matt. 28:18, Phil. 2:9-11). Like Joseph, Jesus with a heart overflowing with mercy, bestows His forgiveness on those who have wronged Him and His Father. Where Joseph's brothers and we deserved only punishment, we received grace instead (Ps. 103:8-11).

We may rightfully fear God. But such fear is unnecessary (1 John 4:18). Through Jesus, we receive God's mercy and compassion. The Bible does not tell us the brothers' reaction to the mercy of Joseph. We can only imagine that their fear was replaced with an exuberant joy and thanksgiving.

Because of Jesus, the joy of having God's mercy is ours. It is a joy that is ours everyday. It is a joy in which we live (Is. 61:7). May the Lord help us to show mercy on others as freely as He has shown mercy on us (Matt. 18:21-34).

Prayer: Lord Jesus, Your mercy and compassion are so much more than I deserve. I could never adequately thank You for all the love You have shown me. Accept my life as a small token of appreciation. Because of You, eternal joy fills my heart. Amen.

Passover Lamb
Rescuer from Death

Readings: Exodus 12:1-13 and 1 Corinthians 5:6-8

Midnight was the time of death. The Lord visited Egypt and brought death to all the firstborn. This included the cattle in the field, the prisoners in the dungeon and even the members of Pharaoh's household (Ex. 12:29). "Pharaoh and all his officials and all the Egyptians got up during the night, and there was loud wailing in Egypt, for there was not a house without someone dead" (Ex. 12: 30).

The only exceptions were the Israelite slaves who trusted in the Lord. God told them ahead of time what would happen and how to avoid His approaching judgment. Trusting in His promise, each Israelite family killed a one-year-old male lamb without defect. They brushed some of its blood on the doorframes of their homes. That evening they ate the roasted lamb along with bitter herbs and unleavened bread (Ex. 12:7-8). As the Lord traveled through Egypt bringing His judgment of death, He "passed over" the homes of the Israelites, which were marked with the blood of the lamb, and spared their lives.

This Old Testament Passover directs us to Jesus, our Paschal Lamb, by whose blood we have eternal life. It is no accident or mere coincidence that when Jesus was given over to death it was during the Passover celebration in Jerusalem (Matt. 26:17-19). Jesus had just finished eating the Seder with His disciples— including the roasted lamb, the bitter herbs, and the unleavened bread—before they went with Him to Gethsemane.

The lambs' blood on the wooden doorframes in Egypt foreshadowed the blood Jesus shed on the wooden cross. The lambs' blood in Egypt saved the Israelites from death; likewise the blood Jesus shed for us saves us from death. That is why He could tell Martha, "I am the resurrection and the life. He who believes in me will live, even though he dies; and whoever lives and believes in Me will never die" (John 11: 25-26).

Yes, Christians still die. But because of the resurrection and the life eternal we have in Jesus, the dominion of death is crushed. Death holds no power over us. Death is not the end of our lives. It is merely a change of address. We need not fear death because we know heaven awaits. Yes, we still mourn the loss of our loved ones—and rightfully so. But the pain of that loss is surpassed by the far greater joy of knowing that we will one day be reunited with our loved ones in heaven.

Referring to all who trust in Him, the Lord speaks through the prophet Hosea saying, "I will ransom them from the power of the grave. Where, O death, are your plagues, Where, O grave, is your destruction" (Hos. 13:14)? St. Paul mentions this passage in 1 Cor. 15:55 then follows with this note of praise, "Thanks be to God! He gives us the victory through our Lord Jesus Christ (1 Cor. 15:57). Jesus has "destroyed death and has brought life and immortality to light through the Gospel" (2 Tim. 1:10).

Prayer: Heavenly Father, sometimes I am frightened by the shadow of death. Remind me that such fear is unnecessary, because Jesus is my Paschal Lamb who was handed over into death for me. He lives so that I too may live forever. Amen.

Pillar of Fire
Beacon of Light

Readings: Exodus 13: 21-22 and John 8:12

In the dark night of the Sinai desert God was there—providing for His people—in a pillar of fire. Through the fire He gave them light and reassured them of His presence. This was not the only time God provided light for His people.

On the first day of creation darkness covered everything (Gen. 1:2). Then God said, "Let there be light" (Gen. 1:3) and immediately there was light. By the power of His almighty Word, He shattered the primeval night and dispelled the gloomy darkness.

That Word is Jesus Christ. St. John tells us, "In the beginning was the Word, and the Word was with God, and the Word was God. He was with God in the beginning. Through Him all things were made; without Him nothing was made that has been made. In Him was life, and that life was the light of men. The light shines in the darkness, but the darkness has not understood it . . . This Word became flesh and made His dwelling among us" (John 1:1- 5, 14).

Jesus told the people, " I am the Light of the world. Whoever follows Me will never walk in darkness, but will have the light of life" (John 8:12). Matthew recognized Jesus' work as the fulfillment of Isaiah's prophecy, "The people living in darkness have seen a great light; on those living in the land of the shadow of death a light has dawned" (Matt. 4:16 and Is. 9:2, cf. Is. 42:16, 60:1-3,19). Jesus lights our way through life like the pillar of fire in the Sinai wilderness.

Jesus came into the world to bring light from above—to dispel the darkness of sin, death, and Satan. Because of Jesus, sin is forgiven (Col. 2:13), death is merely the gate to heaven (Luke 23:43), and Satan is powerless to harm us (Luke 10:17-18, Rev. 20:2). "He can harm us none, He's judged the deed is done; One little word can fell him" (*A Mighty Fortress Is Our God,* stanza 3).

Through faith in Jesus this light is aglow in our hearts. "For God, who said, 'Let light shine out of darkness,' made His light shine in our hearts to give us the light of the knowledge of the glory of God in the face of Christ" (2 Cor. 4:6).

Jesus is the divine light that illuminates our darkest hours. Whatever shadows hang over your life—doubt, fear, or depression— you can say with King David, "You are my lamp, O Lord; the Lord turns my darkness into light" (2 Sam. 22:29). He will guide your way no matter how deep the darkness.

Prayer: Jesus, You are the light of my life. In times of darkness, I look to You to show me the way. Lead me in path of righteousness. When my last hour comes, enlighten the valley of the shadow of death and reassure me of Your loving presence. Amen.

A Piece of Wood
Sweetens the Bitterness

Readings: Exodus: 15:22-27 and Luke 23:33

Sometimes life can be bitter. The children of Israel certainly experienced that during their many years of Egyptian bondage (Ex. 1:11-14). Then after they were freed from slavery, they marched three days into the desert only to find more bitterness at Marah (Ex. 15:23).

Job also knew of life's bitterness. He writes, "If only my anguish could be weighed and all my misery placed on the scales! It would surely outweigh the sands of the seas" (Job 6:2- 3).

What is the bitterness in your life? A financial setback? A prolonged sickness? The death of a loved one? What are you doing about it? The people of Israel complained (Ex. 15:24). That is the most common response. Even Job, proverbially known for his patience, did his share of complaining (Job 19 and 21). It did not help him any.

Complaining is rarely helpful. What did Moses do? "Then Moses cried out to the Lord, and the Lord showed him a piece of wood. He threw it into the water, and the water became sweet" (Ex. 15:25).

Rather than wringing our hands and complaining, let us follow the example of Moses. Let us turn to the Lord. He will help us just as He helped Moses. He also will show us a piece of wood—not just any piece of wood, but—the wooden cross on which Christ died.

The crucifixion of Christ is God's guarantee of His never failing love. Because of Christ, we know that God is with us. He loves us and He will strengthen us no matter what comes our way.

God does not promise to take away life's difficulties. Nor does He promise that we will always understand life's troubles. But He has promised to always be with us, to comfort us, to strengthen us, and to give us the ultimate victory (Ex. 15:1-18; Ps. 27, 46).

If He is with us what can harm us? Or as St. Paul says, "In all things God works for the good of those who love Him. . . . He who did not spare His own Son, but gave Him up for us all—how will He not also, along with Him, graciously give us all things" (Rom. 8:28, 32).

This is why, even though St. Paul knew about the bitterness of life (2 Cor. 11:24-28), he could still write, "Rejoice in the Lord always. I will say it again: Rejoice!" (Phil. 4:4).

This is not a naïve, Pollyanna, optimism—but a faith, which clings firmly to Christ who died on the wooden cross for you. His cross—His death—sweetens life's bitterness.

Prayer: Jesus, I thank You that You are always with me. When bitter times come help me to look to You for my comfort and strength. Sweeten my days with the assurance of Your love. I know You will never disappoint me. Amen.

Manna
Bread of Life

Readings: Exodus 16:14-15, 31 and John 6:48-51

For 40 years the ancient Israelites lived in the Sinai desert. Manna was essential to their survival. They were only in the desert a few weeks before they began to grumble (Ex. 16:1-2). "If only we had died by the Lord's hand in Egypt! There we sat around pots of meat and ate all the food we wanted, but you have brought us out into this desert to starve this entire assembly to death" (Ex. 16:3).

The Lord, in His mercy, heard their complaint. In His love He provided for them. "Thin flakes like frost on the ground appeared on the desert floor. When the Israelites saw it, they said to each other, 'What is it?' For they did not know what it was. Moses said to them, 'It is the bread the LORD has given you to eat' " (Ex. 16: 14-15). In Hebrew, the phrase "What is it?" is pronounced *"Manna."* Thus, the special bread from heaven became known by that name.

This manna reminds us of our Lord, Jesus. As we journey to our promised land, He is essential to our survival. After He miraculously fed the 5,000 with just five small barley loaves and two small fish, he explained to them, "I am the bread of life. Your forefathers ate manna in the desert, yet they died . . . I am the living bread that came down from heaven. If anyone eats of this bread, he will live forever. This bread is My flesh, which I will give for the life of the world . . . I tell you the truth, unless you eat the flesh of the Son of Man and drink His blood, you have no life in you . . . Whoever eats My flesh and drinks My blood remains in Me, and I in him" (John 6:48-56).

Just as manna came from heaven—so did Jesus (John 3:13). Just as manna filled the empty stomachs of the ancient Israelites, so also Jesus fills us when we hunger and thirst for righteousness (Matt. 5:6). Yet, Jesus pointed out a vital difference. All the Israelites who ate manna in the desert eventually died. But all who partake of Jesus and receive Him into their lives through faith will live forever. Christ is our nourishment. Through faith we inwardly and spiritually digest Christ and receive all that he has accomplished for us. Only then can He remain in us and we in Him (John 15:5). Without faith in Christ, we spiritually starve and die.

In the Lord's Supper, along with the bread and the wine, we also receive His body and His blood to eat and to drink. The Israelites took the manna and placed it into their mouths to eat. So also with the Lord's body and blood in the sacrament. It is placed in our mouths to eat and to drink, to feed us with the very body of Christ, which was given up on the cross for us (1 Cor. 11:23-25). This is food that gives us eternal life. It is a foretaste of the feast in heaven when all Christians will gather at the table to partake of the wedding supper of the Lamb (Rev. 19:6-9).

Prayer: O living bread from heaven, I crave the nourishment that only You can give. Feed me with Your body broken on the cross for me, until I feast at the heavenly banquet where I will hunger no more. Amen.

Rock of Massah
Water of Life

Readings: Exodus 17:1-7 and John 19:33-34

The desert was hot and dry. When the children of Israel needed water in the Sinai wilderness, God told Moses, "Strike the rock, and water will come out of it for the people to drink" (Ex. 17:6). Water flowed from the rock and the people could drink their fill. In this way, the Lord provided for those who trusted in Him.

Today we are traveling through a moral and spiritual desert on our way to the Promised Land. So also the Lord has provided for us. After Jesus died on the cross, "one of the soldiers pierced Jesus' side with a spear, bringing a sudden flow of blood and water" (John 19:34). Like the rock of Massah, Jesus was struck for His people.

Like the rock, so also the side of Jesus brought forth water. Jesus, who hung on the cross in thirst (John 19:28), has become the source of living water for all who believe in Him. As Jesus Himself once said, "If anyone is thirsty, let him come to Me and drink. Whoever believes in Me, as the Scripture has said, streams of living water will flow from within him."(John 7:37- 38).

It was Jesus who provided water for the people of Israel from the rock at Massah (1 Cor. 10:3-4). Now this same rock—this same Jesus—provides living water for us. The water of our Baptism brings us life because, like the water from His pierced side, it is united with His promise of blood shed for us. The very life of Christ drained for us at Calvary comes to us in the waters of our Baptism.

Christ is the rock from which flows the baptismal water of life. This water becomes a spring "welling up to eternal life" (John 4:14; Rev. 22:1).

There are many who thirst for the water of life. Let us share with them the Good News of salvation, which flows from Jesus. Only in the Lord will their thirst be quenched.

As He told Isaiah long ago, "The poor and needy search for water, but there is none; their tongues are parched with thirst. But I the LORD will answer them; I, the God of Israel, will not forsake them. I will make rivers flow on barren heights, and springs within the valleys. I will turn the desert into pools of water, and the parched ground into springs" (Is. 41:17-18). This He has done in Jesus Christ. He is the rock that gives living water.

As Moses hid in the clef of a rock to protect himself from the glory of God (Ex. 33:18-23), may we always seek refuge in the wounds of Christ. He is our rock, the cornerstone of our salvation (1 Pet. 2:6-8). He is the foundation on which we live (Eph. 2:19-22). All other ground is sinking sand (Matt. 7:24-27).

"Rock of Ages, cleft for me, Let me hide myself in thee; Let the waters and the blood, From thy riven side which flowed, Be of sin the double cure; Cleanse me from its guilt and stain" (*Rock of Ages,* stanza 1).

Prayer: Oh, Christ, You are the rock of my salvation. Thank You for poring on me Your water of life. Keep me mindful of my Baptism and help me share the Good News with all who thirst. Amen.

Day of Rest
Our Sabbath

Readings: Exodus 20:8-11 and Matthew 11:28

In six days God created the heavens and the earth (Gen. 1). "By the seventh day God had finished the work He had been doing; so on the seventh day He rested from all His work. And God blessed the seventh day and made it holy, because on it He rested from all the work" (Gen. 2:2-3).

Many years later, when God gave the Third Commandment to the ancient Israelites, He recalled His work of creation and His sacred day of rest. Once a week, on the Sabbath Day, the Israelites now were commanded to cease their labors just as God ceased His work after creation.

This was important for two reasons and in each we see the reflection of Christ. First, unlike God, we do tire and grow weary of our labor. Sometimes we may even feel like Job who said, "I have no peace, no quietness; I have no rest, but only turmoil" (Job 3:26). We need a Sabbath, a day of rest. But where do we find such rest—only in the Lord.

King David knew this when he wrote; "My soul finds rest in God alone; my salvation comes from Him" (Ps. 62:1). His son Solomon repeated the wisdom of his father when he said, "Praise be to the Lord, who has given rest to His people Israel just as He promised" (1 Kings 8:56). Then he immediately added, "Not one word has failed of all the good promises He gave through His servant Moses" (1 Kings 8:56).

Solomon knew what gives us true rest—the promises of God— the salvation of God—all of which are enfleshed in Jesus Christ. He is our rest. Christ is our Sabbath! So Jesus Himself could say, "Come to Me, all you who are weary and burdened, and I will give you rest (Matt. 11:28). What burdens you today—sin and guilt from your past—worry and anxiety about your future? There is rest from these when you turn them over to Jesus.

Yet, the Israelites did more than simply rest on the Sabbath. They also recalled the Lord's deliverance. Moses explained to them. "Remember that you were slaves in Egypt and that the Lord your God brought you out of there with a mighty hand and an outstretched arm. Therefore, the Lord your God has commanded you to observe the Sabbath day" (Deut. 5:15).

The Sabbath was a special time to remember their great deliverance. So also, our Sabbath— our day of rest—is a special time to remember our great deliverance in Jesus Christ. On Easter morning Jesus rose from the grave announcing his deliverance for all people. The early Christians were quite right in moving the Day of Rest to the Day of Resurrection. For it is only in His resurrection that we find rest for our weary souls (Col. 2:16-17).

Prayer: Dear Jesus, You rested in the tomb on the Sabbath Day. Help me find rest for my heart and soul. Help me turn all my burdens and worries over to You. Help me find the rest and peace that only You can give. Amen.

The Tabernacle and the Temple
Immanuel

Readings: Exodus 40:34-38 and John 1:1, 14

Where do you look to find God? Where is His dwelling place? Do you search for God among the stars in the sky or in the depths of the sea? Do you look to your inner self to hear His whisper in your quietest thoughts? Or do you think He can be found in popular opinion or majority vote? There is Good News! God does not hide, nor does He wait to be found. He loves us far too much for that. He comes to us.

As the children of Israel wondered through the Sinai desert, their focus of worship was the tabernacle—a large portable tent. That was God's special dwelling place. They did not have to search to find Him. He lived among them (Ex. 25:8). Frequently, the tabernacle was called the "Tent of Meeting" because there God would meet His people. Note that the tabernacle was not a mere symbolic representation of God's presence. It was the actual place of His dwelling. After the tabernacle was built a "cloud covered the Tent of Meeting, and the glory of the Lord filled the tabernacle. . . So the cloud of the Lord was over the tabernacle by day, and fire was in the cloud by night, in the sight of all the house of Israel during all their travels" (Ex. 40:34, 38). What a great comfort it was for the Israelites to look at the Tabernacle and to know God was with them.

Much later in the history of Israel, King Solomon built a more permanent house of worship for the Lord (1 Kings 6). When its construction was complete, it was filled with the glory of the Lord. "When the priests withdrew from the Holy Place, the cloud filled the temple of the LORD. And the priests could not perform their service because of the cloud, for the glory of the LORD filled his temple. Then Solomon said, 'The LORD has said that He would dwell in a dark cloud; I have indeed built a magnificent temple for you, a place for you to dwell forever' " (1 Kings 8:10-13). This temple as beautiful as it was did not last forever. The Babylonians destroyed it in 586 B.C. (2 Kings 25:8-9). How the people must have wept to see the dwelling place of God destroyed. How would God now dwell in their midst? A greater temple was to come (Ezek. 37:27-28, Is 7:14).

"Then the Jews demanded of Him, 'What miraculous sign can You show us to prove Your authority to do all this?' Jesus answered them, 'Destroy this temple, and I will raise it again in three days.' The Jews replied, 'It has taken forty-six years to build this temple, and You are going to raise it in three days?' But the temple He had spoken of was his body" (John 2:18-21).

Just as God dwelled in the tabernacle and in the temple, so also He dwells in the man, Jesus of Nazareth. As St. John records in his prologue, "In the beginning was the Word, and the Word was with God, and the Word was God. . . . The Word became flesh and made His dwelling among us" (John 1:1, 14). In Jesus, God dwells with us (Matt. 1:23, Rev. 21:3-4). If you want to find God, look to Jesus.

Prayer: Immanuel, I thank You that You have revealed God to me. Because of You, I do not need to look for God in all the mysteries of the universe. But to know God, I look to You. Help me to remain focused on You always. Amen.

Day of Atonement
Takes Away Our Sins

Readings: Leviticus 16:20-22 and John 1:29

Special worship services were important for the children of Israel even as they traveled through the desert. Once a year on the Day of Atonement (Yom Kipper), the high priest was allowed to enter the Most Holy Place—the most sacred part of the tabernacle.

There he would sprinkle blood on the ark of the covenant (a wooden chest overlaid with gold). In this way, atonement would be made for the sins of the people (Lev. 16:15-17). This blood is a reminder of the blood Jesus would shed for us on Calvary's cross to atone (or pay) for our sins.

In the Greek translation of the Old Testament, there was a technical term used to refer to the lid on the ark. It is frequently translated as "atonement cover" (Lev. 16:13, 14, 15) or "sacrifice of atonement." St. Paul chose to use that very same Greek word to refer to Jesus when he wrote; "God presented Him [Jesus] as a 'sacrifice of atonement' [or atonement cover]" (Rom. 3:25). Jesus, stained with His own blood, is the atonement cover for our sins. The first Good Friday is our Day of Atonement. That was the day all our sins were taken away.

After the high priest sprinkled the blood on the atonement cover, he would return outside. There he would lay both his hands on the head of a live goat and confess all the sins of the people. In that way their sins would be placed upon the goat. Then the goat would be released into the desert. "The goat will carry on itself all their sins to a solitary place" (Lev. 16:22).

Through the means of this scapegoat, God removed the sins of the people. Here again is another picture of the work of Jesus on Good Friday. As the Old Testament prophet Isaiah said, "The Lord has laid on Him the iniquity of us all" (Is. 53: 6). So also John the Baptizer said, "Look, the Lamb of God, who takes away the sin of the world" (John 1:29). God placed upon Jesus all the sins of the world. As the Old Testament scapegoat was sent into the desert, so Christ was sent to Calvary, bearing our sins to atone for each and every one. There on the cross His heavenly Father turned His back on Him (Matt. 27:46) so that He would never turn His back on us (Deut. 31:6, Heb. 13:5).

Because of Jesus our sins are removed. "As far as the east is from the west, so far has He removed our transgressions from us" (Ps. 103:12). We no longer need to feel guilty about our past however grievous it might be. All our sins are taken away. Our guilt is gone forever. Through His death He paid the debt we owe—a debt we could never repay (Matt. 18:23-26). "He is the atoning sacrifice for our sins, and not only for ours but also for the sins of the whole world" (1 John 2:2).

Prayer: Jesus, You have freed me from the burden of my sin. Even though I do not deserve Your blessings, You received my sins upon Yourself and You took the punishment that I deserved. You shed Your blood for me. Thank You. Amen.

Year of Jubilee
Liberator

Readings: Leviticus 25:39-41 and Luke 4:16-21

For ancient Israel every fiftieth year was a year of Jubilee. They were to, "Consecrate the fiftieth year and proclaim liberty throughout the land to all its inhabitants" (Lev. 25:10). These words (which are inscribed on the cracked Liberty Bell in Philadelphia) remind us that true emancipation comes from the Lord.

During this time of Jubilee, debts were forgiven, and slaves released. It was a time of great joy and celebration. The year of Jubilee began on the Day of Atonement (Lev. 25:9) after the High Priest offered the sacrifice to atone for the sins of all the people (Lev. 16). How appropriate then that on the year of Jubilee the people, empowered by the very grace they had received, would then also forgive those who were indebted to them (Matt. 18:21-35). Being liberated from their sins, they could now share that liberation with others.

Surely the prophet Isaiah had the year of Jubilee in mind when he wrote, "The Spirit of the Sovereign LORD is on me, because the LORD has anointed me to preach good news to the poor. He has sent me to bind up the brokenhearted, to proclaim freedom for the captives and release from darkness for the prisoners, to proclaim the year of the LORD's favor" (Is. 61:1-2). But did Isaiah only have in mind a one-year Jubilee? Or did he have in mind something more—an eternal Jubilee—a never-ending liberation brought about by the Lord Himself?

In His first sermon in His hometown, Jesus quoted this passage from Isaiah, then to the amazement of His hearers he added, "Today, this scripture is fulfilled in your hearing" (Luke 4:21). Here Jesus is linking the Old Testament with the New Testament. He is uniting the Year of Jubilee—and all the joy and liberation it contained—with His very own ministry! The work of Jesus inaugurates a Jubilee celebration that has no end!

In Him all who are bound by the shackles of hate find their liberation. All who are oppressed by sorrow find their emancipation. All who are tormented by chaos find their release. "A man is slave to whatever has mastered him" (2 Pet. 2:19). But in Christ there is freedom from all that would enslave us (John 8:36). How are we to live in this ongoing Jubilee? We live like the Israelites who, following the Day of Atonement, shared their liberation with others.

We share our freedom in Christ with those who are still oppressed. As St. Paul wrote, "It is for freedom that Christ has set us free. Stand firm, then, and do not let yourselves be burdened again by a yoke of slavery . . . .You, my brothers, were called to be free. But do not use your freedom to indulge the sinful nature; rather, serve one another in love" (Gal. 5:1-13). May you live in the freedom of Christ—an eternal Jubilee— now and always.

Prayer: O Lord, just as You liberated the children of Israel from the bondage of the Egyptians, so You have liberated me from the bondage of my sins. Help me to always share this liberation by forgiving others as You have forgiven me. Amen.

Family Friend
Redeemer

Readings: Leviticus 25:47-49 and 1 Peter 1:18-19

An Israelite who was unable to pay a debt could sell himself into slavery and work for his creditor to pay off the amount he owed. However, he could be redeemed from his servitude and freed from his debt if any family member paid the debt for him. Such a family member would be a true friend indeed.

You and I owed God a tremendous debt. We needed to pay the penalty for our sins. We owe God for our lack of love both to Him and to our neighbor (Mark 12:28-30). This loveless attitude shows itself in our laziness, our short tempers, our evil thoughts, our pride, and our jealously. We see it in all the wrong we have ever done and all the good we have failed to do. We sin daily and the debt we incur is infinite and immeasurable. The law of God demands restitution. But it is a debt we can never pay.

Because of this debt, we deserve nothing from God but His eternal wrath and punishment (Eph. 2:3). He will not put off His wrath forever. The day of God's wrath is coming (Zeph. 1:14-18). Our only hope is expressed in the words of the psalmist who writes, "Rise up and help us; redeem us because of Your unfailing love" (Ps. 44:26).

God has heard the pleas of His people. He promised that a redeemer would come, "The Redeemer will come to Zion, to those in Jacob who repent of their sins, declares the LORD" (Is. 59:20). But our debt is so great who can this redeemer be? Who can possible pay the vast amount we owe?

The Old Testament prophets tell us. Isaiah writes, "You will drink the milk of nations and be nursed at royal breasts. Then you will know that I, the LORD, am your Savior, your Redeemer, the Mighty One of Jacob" (Is. 60:16). Jeremiah also said, "Yet their Redeemer is strong; the LORD Almighty is His name" (Jer. 50:34).

God Himself promised to be our relative—our family friend— who will pay the price to redeem us. So He became incarnate and was born of the Virgin Mary. "But when the time had fully come, God sent His Son, born of a woman, born under law, to redeem those under law" (Gal. 4:4-5). He paid the price by taking upon Himself the suffering and the condemnation we deserved because of our sin. "Christ redeemed us from the curse of the law by becoming a curse for us" (Gal. 3:13-14).

He took our punishment and redeemed us with His own precious blood. St. Peter explains, "For you know that it was not with perishable things such as silver or gold that you were redeemed from the empty way of life handed down to you from your forefathers, but with the precious blood of Christ, a lamb without blemish or defect" (1 Pet. 1:18-19).

Prayer: Oh Lord I am Yours twice over. In the first place You created me, then second You also redeemed me with Your precious blood. In times of doubt or worry, help me to remember that I belong to You and You will always take care of me. Amen.

Bronze Serpent
Nehushtan

Readings: Numbers 21: 4-9 and John 3:14

Snakes have a bad reputation. It goes back all the way to Adam and Eve. Satan used a snake to tempt Eve (Gen. 3:1-6). Since then all humanity has been inflicted with the venom of Satan and subject to sin and death (Rom. 5:12). When God gave Moses the list of unclean foods, which the Israelites were not to eat, snakes were on the list. He made it very clear saying, "You are not to eat any creature that moves about on the ground, whether it moves on its belly or walks on all fours or on many feet; it is detestable" (Lev. 11:42). For ancient Israel, snakes were vile, disgusting, and loathsome.

Yet, at one time, God purposely inflicted His people with an abundance of these abhorrent creatures. After the Lord freed them from Egyptian bondage, the Israelites complained about their situation in the desert. "Why have you brought us up out of Egypt to die in the desert? There is no bread! There is no water! And we detest this miserable food!" (Num. 21:4-5). They had turned away from the Lord. To bring them back to His loving care it would be difficult and painful—not for Him, but—for them (Heb. 12:10- 11).

God sent poisonous snakes that bit them and killed many (Num. 21:6; confer 1 Cor. 10:9-11). The people repented and "The LORD said to Moses, 'Make a snake and put it up on a pole; anyone who is bitten can look at it and live.' So Moses made a bronze snake and put it up on a pole. Then when anyone was bitten by a snake and looked at the bronze snake, he lived" (Num. 21:8-9).

The people were healed by looking at the brass image of the vile, unclean snake lifted above them. Seven hundred years after Moses, king Hezekiah destroyed the bronze serpent. It was called Nehushtan (2 Kings 18:4). The word "Nehushtan" is not only a combination of the Hebrew words for "snake" and "bronze", but it also sounds very similar to the Hebrew word meaning "unclean thing."

Jesus told Nicodemus, "Just as Moses lifted up the snake in the desert, so the Son of Man must be lifted up, that everyone who believes in Him may have eternal life" (John 3:14). This bronze snake on the pole reminds us of the "unclean thing" who once hung on the cross for us. Jesus became an unclean thing to destroy the power of the ancient serpent—Satan (Gen. 3:15, Rev. 12:9). "God made Him who had no sin to be sin for us" (2 Cor. 5:21). Jesus bore our sins (1 Pet. 2:24) and took upon Himself God's curse (Gal. 3:13). Jesus became like a serpent or a worm scorned and despised by the people (Ps. 22:6). His heavenly Father considered Him repulsive (Matt. 27:46).

In his explanation of John 3, Martin Luther calls Christ "our Serpent of Salvation." Christ is our Nehushtan. He became an unclean thing for us so that all who look up to Him can be healed. To this very day, the caduceus (two snakes twisted around a pole) is a universal sign for healing. May we look to Jesus to heal our every ill in body and soul.

Prayer: Christ Jesus, You are my Nehushtan. Lifted up on the cross, You became an unclean thing when You took my sins upon Yourself. May I always look up to You for the divine healing that only You can give. Amen.

Moses
Deliverer

Readings: Deuteronomy 18:15 and John 6:14

In the Old Testament figure of Moses, we see a beautiful picture of Jesus. Even as children they both had their enemies who sought their deaths. Moses was born at a time when the Egyptian Pharaoh feared the Israelites. Although they were slaves, they had grown to become a formidable and threatening group (Ex. 1:8- 13).

Eventually the pharaoh decided to drown all the newborn Hebrew boys into the Nile (Ex. 1:22). This would have been the end of Moses if his mother and sister had not placed him in a basket and hidden him in the river where the Egyptian princes later found him (Ex. 2:1-6).

The situation was similar with the infant Jesus and Herod the Great. When Herod heard from the Wise Men that a new king was born, he immediately felt threatened. This fear led him to order the murder of all the young boys in Bethlehem (Matt. 2:16). But with the help of his family, Jesus escaped to Egypt (Matt. 2:13). Thus Jesus, just as ancient Israel, was "called out of Egypt" (Hos. 11:1, Matt. 2:15).

Moses grew up and became a great prophet who proclaimed a message of freedom (Ex. 5:1). The validity of his message was divinely confirmed with numerous miracles (Ex. 7-11). The same was true of Jesus. He too grew up to be a great prophet (Luke 7:16), who proclaimed freedom for his people (Luke 4:18, Gal 5:1). His message also was divinely confirmed with many miracles (John 14:11). Yet, in spite of the miracles, both Moses (Acts 7:25, 39) and Jesus (John 1:11; Mark 15:12-13) were rejected by some of their own people.

Yet, such rejections did not deter them in their work of deliverance. By God's grace, Moses still successfully delivered the children of Israel from Egyptian slavery.

When he raised his hands, the Red Sea parted so the children of Israel could walk across on dry ground (Ex. 14:21-22). After 430 years of slavery, they finally were delivered from the hand of their enemies. The horses and chariots of pharaoh were completely destroyed (Ex. 14:28).

Likewise, our Lord Jesus lifted His hands to be nailed to the cross. There on the cross our Lord Jesus delivered us from our greatest enemies—sin, death, and Satan. Just as the Egyptians held the children of Israel in bondage, so also did the depravity of sin, the fear of death, and the power of Satan hold us captive. But Jesus, just as Moses before Him, won deliverance for His people.

Because of Jesus, we are delivered from the power, the threat, and the terror of our fiercest enemies. He, who was delivered into the hands of His enemies (Luke 24:7), has provided us ultimate deliverance from our enemies.

Prayer: Heavenly Father, I thank You that through Moses You delivered the ancient Israelites from the power of the Egyptians, but I offer You even greater thanks that You sent Your only Son into the world to deliver me from all that would enslave me. Amen.

Samson (1)
Miraculously Born

Readings: Judges 13:1-5 and Luke 1:26-35

Manoah's wife was sad. She was unable to have children. Then one day an angel appeared and told her that in spite of her condition, she would become pregnant and give birth to a son (Judg. 13:3). Mary, the mother of Jesus was in a similar situation. She too was unable to give birth because of her virginity.

Yet, just as with Manoah's wife, so also with Joseph's betrothed, an angel of the Lord appeared and announced that Mary would miraculously conceive and give birth to a son (Luke 1:26-35). In Samson's miraculous conception and birth we begin to see a picture of the first Christmas.

Samson was not like the other children. He was different—set apart. The angel told his mother, "The boy is to be a Nazirite, set apart to God from birth" (Judg. 13:5). The word "Nazirite" is from the Hebrew word that means, "dedicated" or "separated."

Being separate and different from the others, Samson would lead a special life. The angel continued, "He will begin the deliverance of Israel from the hands of the Philistines" (Judg. 13:5).

Here the similarity with Jesus is developed further. Jesus also was set apart from birth. He will be different from the others. How will He be different? He will save us from our enemies—even our worst enemies—sin (Matt.

1:21), death (John 11:25-26) and the power of Satan (Luke 10:17-19).

Samson also had special power. He was blessed with tremendous physical strength (Judg. 16:3). No ropes, however strong, could bind him (Judg. 15:14). He could kill a thousand men using only the jawbone of a donkey (Judg. 15:15). His strength was the envy of his enemies (Judg. 16:5).

Jesus was also endowed with great power. He had the power to heal the sick (Luke 6:19), calm storms (Luke 8:22-25), and even raise the dead (Luke 7:11-17). But his greatest power is the ability to forgive sins (Mark 2:1-12). His power is all we need. As Peter says, "His divine power has given us everything we need for life and godliness" (2 Pet. 1:3).

To be sure Samson had his faults (Judg. 16:1). Nevertheless, he was a special man, chosen by God to lead His people. For 20 years, he led the people of Israel (Judg. 15:20). His miraculous birth, his special dedication, and his great power all point us to an even Greater One, who was miraculously born for you.

Prayer: Heavenly Father, in Your infinite wisdom, You chose Samson to deliver your people from their enemies. May his miraculous birth, dedication to Your purpose, and his tremendous power always remind me of Jesus. Amen.

Samson's Riddle
The Lion's Carcass

Readings: Judges 14:1-14 and Revelation 5:1-5

"Out of the eater, something to eat; out of the strong, something sweet" (Judg. 14:14). What is it? Who is this strong eater? And what sweetness does he give? What an odd riddle.

It had Samson's companions stumped for days. Finally, after threatening her, they got the answer from Samson's bride. Then they reported to him, "What is sweeter than honey? What is stronger than a lion?" (Judg. 14:18). They had their answer—a honeycomb in the mouth of a dead lion.

In some ancient Jewish writings, the Messiah is portrayed as a powerful lion. In the last days, He will come to judge some and have mercy on others. [Louis Brighton, *Revelation* (St. Louis: Concordia Publishing House, 1999), 136]. That is a vivid portrayal of our Lord Jesus. It is true that He was humble (Matt. 11:29). It is true that He was led to the slaughter like a lamb (Is. 53:7, Matt. 27:31). By all outward appearances, He looked weak. But He was not.

Quite to the contrary, with the strength of the most ferocious lion, He fought Satan and rose victorious. Our Lord devoured His enemies. All who are against the Lord will be torn apart. He is ferocious. As He told Israel, "Like a lion I will devour them" (Hos. 13:8). So also St. John referring to Jesus writes, "Do not weep! See, the Lion of the tribe of Judah, . . . has triumphed" (Rev. 5:5).

The lion in Samson's riddle was only a carcass. So also was our Lord Jesus—for a time. His lifeless body was taken down from the cross and His mouth no longer spoke the sweet message of the Gospel—at least for three days.

Then, once again after His resurrection, words sweeter than honey flowed from His mouth— words of love, peace, and forgiveness. "How sweet are Your words to my taste, sweeter than honey to my mouth" (Ps. 119:103). No bitter words of anger, hate, or deception ever came from His mouth (1 Pet. 2:22-23).

Samson's companions were concerned about the riddle because there was so much hanging in the balance—30 linen garments and 30 sets of clothes (Judg. 14:12-13). So also in knowing Jesus— there is much hanging in the balance—yes, a whole new wardrobe. Those who know that Jesus has torn apart His enemies— those who have tasted and digested the sweet Gospel He taught—those who know Jesus and what He has done for them— are clothed in His righteousness (Rev. 7:13-14).

Our only response can be one of sheer delight, "I delight greatly in the Lord; my soul rejoices in my God. For He has clothed me with garments of salvation and arrayed me in a robe of righteousness" (Is. 61:10).

Prayer: Oh Lion of Judah, it is no riddle or puzzle to know You. You have devoured your enemies. Yet, the words of Gospel, which proceed from Your mouth, are sweeter than honey. Keep me clothed in Your righteousness always. Amen.

Samson (2)
Victorious in Battle

Readings: Judges 15:12-17 and 1 Corinthians 15:56-57

Samson was a valiant warrior. He knew what it was like to stand up to powerful enemies, fight against tremendous odds, and finish victoriously. He could kill a lion with his bear hands (Judg. 14:5- 6), catch 300 foxes (Judg. 15:4), and kill 1,000 enemies with the jawbone of a donkey (Judg. 15:15-16). Samson was no stranger to fighting hard and being victorious against both man and beast.

We also have numerous enemies. St. Paul writes, "For our struggle is not against flesh and blood, but against the . . . powers of this dark world and against the spiritual forces of evil in the heavenly realms" (Eph. 6:12). These enemies are formidable. The evil in this world and the satanic forces from Hell have formed a coalition to bring about our eternal defeat. Either they must be vanquished or we will be eternally doomed. But how can we conquer the overwhelming power of evil? On our own we are quite helpless.

There is only one, who, with Samson-like strength, defeated our enemies. Zechariah speaks of Him when he says, "Praise be to the Lord, the God of Israel, because . . . He has raised up a horn of salvation for us in the house of His servant David (as he said through His holy prophets of long ago), salvation from our enemies and from the hand of all who hate us . . . to rescue us from the hand of our enemies, and to enable us to serve Him without fear" (Luke 1:68-74).

This One is Jesus. This is the One King David speaks of when he says, "The Lord [*the Father*] says to my Lord [*His Son*]: 'Sit at my right hand until I make your enemies a footstool for your feet' . . . you will rule in the midst of your enemies" (Ps. 110:1-2).

After Jesus was baptized, He went "into the desert to be tempted by the devil" (Matt. 4:1). Jesus was the aggressor. He actively sought out His enemy so He could engage him in battle. Jesus was tempted to use His divine power for His own needs (Matt. 4:3-4). He was tempted to use His power to test the loving care of His Father (Matt. 4:5-7). He was tempted to forsake His mission and go in league with Satan (Matt. 4:8-10). There were still other temptations (Luke 4:13). But Jesus conquered them all (1 Pet. 2:22, Heb. 4:15).

In conquering all temptations, He conquered the Tempter—for you. Jesus has defeated evil. He has conquered the power of sin. We can say with David, "How awesome are Your deeds! So great is Your power that Your enemies cringe before You" (Ps. 66:3). Life can be frightening. The terrible power of evil is real, and it must be taken seriously. But we need not fear. Rather, "Thanks be to God! He gives us the victory through our Lord Jesus Christ" (1 Cor. 15:57).

Prayer: Lord, in the face of evil I am weak and powerless. But I need not fear, because You have fought the good fight. You have battled evil and won. You have conquered the enemies of sin and Satan. Keep me mindful that in You the victory is mine. Amen.

Samson (3)
Victorious in Death

Readings: Judges 16:23-30 and Hebrews 2:14

The secret to Samson's God-given great strength was his long hair (Judg. 16:17). Yes, that is an odd way to give physical strength to Samson, but who are we to question the means God chooses to accomplish His work (1 Pet. 3:21)?

Samson loved Delilah (Judg. 16:4). But one thing he did not like about her was her constant nagging (Judg.16:16). She wanted to know the secret of his great strength, but he refused to tell her. Three different times he pretended to tell her only to tease her (Judg. 16:6-15). Finally, her nagging wore him down, and he told her the truth (Judg. 16:17).

That was to be the greatest mistake of his life. She, whom Samson loved, then betrayed him, and handed him over to his captors in return for a considerable amount of silver (Judg. 16:5, 18). They immediately cut his hair and carried him away to be mocked and brutally mistreated (Judg. 16:21, 25).

Our Lord Jesus received similar treatment. Like Samson, Jesus was betrayed by one he loved, and handed over to his enemies for a payment of silver. Judas knew where Jesus would be on Maundy Thursday (John 18:2). For 30 silver coins he led the captors to the Garden of Gethsemane and betrayed Jesus with a kiss (Matt. 26:14-15, 47-49).

After Jesus was arrested, he was cruelly mocked and beaten (Mark 15:16-20).

In captivity, Samson's hair began to grow out (Judg. 16:22). During a great celebration, the Philistines asked for Samson to be brought out so they might be entertained by his great feats of strength (Judg. 16:25). One of the servants placed Samson between two supporting pillars of the temple. Samson prayed, "O Sovereign LORD, remember me. O God, please strengthen me just once more" (Judg. 16:28). Then with arms outstretched, "He pushed with all his might, and down came the temple on the rulers and all the people in it. Thus, he killed more people when he died than while he lived" (Judg. 16:30). What a great victory for Samson! Even though it cost him his life.

Jesus' greatest victory also cost Him His life. With arms outstretched, he was nailed to Calvary's cross, and His death brought the ultimate defeat of all His enemies. While Jesus was dying on the cross, He did not look victorious, but He was winning the most important battle in the history of the world—the final battle against death and the devil. "Since the children have flesh and blood, He too shared in their humanity so that by His death He might destroy him who holds the power of death—that is the devil" (Heb. 2:14). The glorious announcement of victory was made on Easter, but the decisive battle was fought and won on Good Friday—for you.

Prayer: Dear Jesus, how much You must love me. You allowed Yourself to be beaten, mocked and crucified so that You could conquer my greatest fears—sin, death, and the devil. Thank You for Your great love. Help me to treasure it always. Amen.

David (1)
King of Kings

Readings: 2 Samuel 7:16 and Matthew 27:11

God made a very special promise to David. The Lord told him, "When your days are over and you rest with your fathers, I will raise up your offspring to succeed you, who will come from your own body. . . . Your house and your kingdom will endure forever before Me; your throne will be established forever" (2 Sam. 7:12- 16).

What a marvelous promise. Here King David had God's promise that David's kingdom will have no end. David's offspring will rule forever. In world history, kingdoms come and go. Family dynasties last for several generations, then they are overturned by a foreign power or a different family in their own country. But God says to David, "Not so with your family—it will rule forever. Its kingdom will have no end."

This promise was so precious to David and his ancient people that they even put it to song. Psalm 89 declares, "I will sing of the Lord's great love forever . . . You said, 'I have made a covenant with My chosen one, I have sworn to David My servant, 'I will establish your line forever and make your throne firm through all generations . . . I will not violate My covenant . . . and I will not lie to David . . . his line will continue forever and his throne [will] endure before Me like the sun" (Ps. 89:1, 3, 4, 34, 35, 36). Yet, many found cause to doubt this great promise.

In 586 B.C. the Babylonians conquered Judah, crushed Jerusalem, and took its people captive. David's great empire was gone! The reign of David's family tree was over! Like a giant oak it fell with a thunderous crash, and there was nothing left but a stump of its former glory. But those who listened to Isaiah had hope. Because he assured them that they had not seen the end of the Davidic dynasty. "For to us a child is born, . . . Of the increase of His government and peace there will be no end. He will reign on David's throne and over his kingdom, establishing and upholding it with justice and righteousness from that time on and forever (Is. 9:7).

Or in other words, "A shoot will come up from the stump of Jesse; from his roots a Branch will bear fruit." (Is. 11:1) And who is that branch? The Hebrew word for "branch" (also used in Zech. 6:12-13) sounds very similar to the word for "Nazarene." The branch is the Nazarene. So Matt. 2:23 tells us that Jesus grew up "in a town called Nazareth. So it was fulfilled what was said through the prophets: 'He will be called a Nazarene.'"

Contrary to all outward appearances, with the fall of Jerusalem to the Babylonians, the Davidic dynasty did not come to an end. It merely began to pave the way for David's greater Son—Jesus of Nazareth. He is the heir of David who will reign forever. Of His kingdom there will be no end. "The kingdom of the world has become the kingdom of our Lord and of His Christ, and He will reign for ever and ever" (Rev. 11:15).

Prayer: I thank You Lord that You did not forget Your promise to king David. But you kept it through Jesus in a greater way than anyone could have imagined. Keep me mindful Lord, that all of Your promises are fulfilled in Christ. Amen.

Solomon (1)
Teacher of Wisdom

Readings: 1 Kings 4:29-34 and Colossians 2:2-3

The proverbial wisdom of Solomon has been known throughout the ages—and rightly so. God promised him, "I will give you a wise and discerning heart, so that there will never have been anyone like you, nor will there ever be" (1 Kings 3:12). God kept His promise (as He keeps all His promises).

"God gave Solomon wisdom and very great insight, and a breadth of understanding as measureless as the sand on the seashore" (1 Kings 4:29). The news of Solomon's great wisdom spread to other countries. People from all over the world came to listen to him (1 Kings 10:24).

One foreign leader who came to see him was the queen of Sheba. She "talked with him about everything that was on her mind. Solomon answered all her questions; nothing was too hard for the king to explain to her . . . She was overwhelmed" (1 Kings 10:2- 3, 5). It is no wonder that we still are impressed with the wisdom of Solomon to this very day.

This divine wisdom, which Solomon had in abundance, became incarnate in Jesus Christ. St. Paul explains, "Where is the wise man? Where is the scholar? Where is the philosopher of this age? Has not God made foolish the wisdom of the world? For since in the wisdom of God the world through its wisdom did not know Him, God was pleased through the foolishness of what was preached to save those who believe. Jews demand miraculous signs and Greeks look for wisdom, but we preach Christ crucified: a stumbling block to Jews and foolishness to Gentiles, but to those whom God has called, both Jews and Greeks, Christ is the power of God and the wisdom of God. . . . It is because of Him that you are in Christ Jesus, who has become for us wisdom from God that is, our righteousness, holiness and redemption. Therefore, as it is written: 'Let him who boasts boast in the Lord'" (1 Cor. 1:20-24, 30).

Solomon himself wrote, "Wisdom is more precious than rubies, and nothing you desire can compare with her" (Prov. 8:11). If that is true concerning human wisdom, then how much more that is true with respect to Christ!

Only Christ, the wisdom of God in the flesh, can teach us about life, forgiveness, and salvation—eternal things— the knowledge of which will continue even in heaven, long after all earthly knowledge has faded away. Christ is both the teacher and the subject.

If the Queen of Sheba was impressed with the wisdom of Solomon, then how much more should we be impressed with Jesus? As He told the Pharisees, "now one greater than Solomon is here" (Matt. 12:42).

Prayer: Heavenly Father, the apostle James writes, "If any of you lacks wisdom, he should ask God, . . . and it will be given to him" (James 1:5). I am asking you now Lord, give me Your wisdom from above— the wisdom that only comes from Your Son Jesus. Amen.

Elijah
Ascended Into Heaven

Readings: 2 Kings 2:9-13 and Acts 1:6-11

Elijah's work was finished. It was time for God to call him home. His great disciple Elisha knew what was about to happen, but he did not want to talk about it (2 Kings 2:3). After the two walked together for quite some distance, Elijah finally suggests that they should split apart and go their separate ways.

He knew his departure was imminent. Yet, Elisha refused saying, "As surely as the Lord lives and as you live, I will not leave you" (2 Kings 2:6). This is the same attitude of faithful persistence we see in Thomas (John 11:16) and Peter (Luke 22:33). May the Lord give us all such an attitude.

Finally, "Elijah said to Elisha, 'Tell me, what can I do for you before I am taken from you?' 'Let me inherit a double portion of your spirit,' Elisha replied" (2 Kings 2:9). Here Elisha was not asking for a ministry greater than his master's. Rather, according to the Law of Deut. 21:17, he was merely asking to follow in his master's steps. He wanted the ability to carry on his teacher's work. "'You have asked a difficult thing.' Elijah said, 'yet if you see me when I am taken from you, it will be yours—otherwise not'" (2 Kings 2:10).

Soon after that a fiery chariot with horses appeared and separated the two men. Elisha felt a mighty wind and saw the chariot carry his master up to heaven. He knew he would follow in his master's footsteps.

Just as Elisha saw his master miraculously taken into heaven so also the 11 disciples witnessed Jesus' ascension. These impressive departures did not take place for Jesus and Elijah, but for the benefit of those, left behind, who would carry on in their master's steps. What a boost to their faith—to witness such an event! In both cases, the miraculous ascensions gave divine confirmation to their faith and their future ministry.

Elisha followed in the spirit of Elijah. So also on Pentecost, 10 days after the ascension, the disciples were given the Spirit of Jesus to empower them to carry on His work. Embolden with His Holy Spirit, the disciples no longer cowered behind locked doors (John 20:19). They were seen publicly, healing and teaching in his name (Acts 2 and 3). This is the same Spirit He has given us so we too can have the courage to carry on His work (2 Tim. 1:7).

As Elijah ascended into heaven he left behind his cloak. There was nothing special about the cloak itself. But God worked through that cloak in a miraculous way (2 Kings 2:13-14). So also when Jesus ascended into heaven, He left behind His most precious sacraments. By themselves the water of Baptism or the bread and wine in the Lord's Supper are nothing special. But God also works through them to do miraculous things. Through them He gives us forgiveness (Matt. 26:28) and new life (Rom. 6:3-4).

Prayer: Lord Jesus, when You ascended into heaven You withdrew Your physical presence from us. Yet, You also promised to be with us always. Help me to recognize Your loving and powerful presence in Your precious Word and sacraments. Amen.

Solomon (2)
Prince of Peace

Readings: 1 Chronicles 22:7-9 and John 14:27

King David wanted to build a beautiful temple for the Lord, but God said no. David saw much conflict and bloodshed in his life. Even from the days of his youth David was a soldier (1 Sam. 17). He fought and conquered foreign enemies (2 Sam. 8:1-14), as well as those from his own household (2 Sam. 18). He would not be the one to build the Lord's house. For this prestigious assignment God would chose David's son—Solomon.

This name, which the Lord himself chose, is from the Hebrew word "Shalom" which means "peace" (1 Chron. 22:9). Unlike his father David, Solomon would be a man of peace. During Solomon's reign, the neighboring countries did not even think of invading (they paid him tribute, 1 Kings 4:21), and everyone dwelled in safety (1 Kings 4: 25).

As Solomon brought peace to Israel, so Jesus brings peace to all humankind. Jesus is the real Prince of Peace as Isaiah foretold, "For to us a child is born, to us a son is given, and the government will be on His shoulders. And He will be called Wonderful Counselor, Mighty God, Everlasting Father, Prince of Peace. Of the increase of His government and peace there will be no end" (Is. 9:6-7).

Jesus came to us to bring us a peace that surpasses all our understanding (Phil. 4:7). His peace surpasses our understanding because its origin—in His perfect life and death for us—cannot be grasped or understood by our rational minds. Because of its divine origin, this peace from Christ cannot be destroyed by anything. There is no person or power or situation in this world— there is no satanic force from beyond this world—that can take away the peace that Jesus gives you.

Sometimes life is not so peaceful. Chaos seems to reign. Confusion, anger, disappointment, and frustration—all work together to dethrone the Prince of Peace. But they can't. No matter what turmoil is in your life, you have an inner tranquility and serenity that can never be taken away. Because you have the Prince of Peace, and He will never leave you or forsake you (Deut. 31:6). No matter how out of control your life may seem, Jesus is in control and He loves you. He is your peace (Eph. 2:14).

Jesus knew His crucifixion would be difficult for Him and His disciples. On the evening of Maundy Thursday, He began to prepare them by giving them His peace. "Peace I leave with you, My peace I give you . . . do not be afraid" (John 14:27). So He also prepares us, for whatever turmoil our future holds—by giving us His peace. As St. Paul explains, "Do not be anxious about anything, but in everything, by prayer and petition, with thanksgiving, present your requests to God. And the peace of God which transcends all understanding, will guard your hearts and your minds in Christ Jesus" (Phil. 4:6-7).

Prayer: Dear Jesus, bring Your peace into my life. In times of chaos and confusion, remind me that You are in control. Help me to always find comfort and assurance in your loving embrace. Amen.

Solomon (3)
King of Glory

Readings: 2 Chronicles 9:13-28 and Matthew 13:44-46

The glorious wealth of Solomon's kingdom was awesome to behold. He received 25 tons of gold annually (1 Kings 10:14). His throne was inlaid with ivory and gold. All the royal goblets were gold. Silver was so common it was not even used. Solomon owned hundreds of chariots and thousands of horses. Scripture tells us, "Solomon was greater in riches . . . than all the other kings of the earth" (1 Kings 10:23).

Solomon certainly was a king who reigned in great glory. But he was only a brief glimpse of a King who reigns in even greater glory—our Lord Jesus. How much is His kingdom worth? Jesus Himself tells us, "The kingdom of heaven is like treasure hidden in a field. When a man found it, he hid it again, and then in his joy went and sold all he had and bought that field" (Matt. 13:44). The kingdom over which Jesus reigns is worth far more than gold or silver. It cost the Son of God His very life—His body broken on the cross for you—His blood, shed on the cross for you. You have a place in His kingdom by believing in Him.

The queen of Sheba was reluctant to believe the news of Solomon's great wealth. She said, "The report I heard in my own country about your achievements . . . is true. But I did not believe these things until I came and saw with my own eyes. Indeed, not even half was told me; in . . . wealth you have far exceeded the report I heard" (1 Kings 10:6-7).

So also, when Thomas heard the good news of Jesus' resurrection, he was so doubtful. "Unless I see the nail marks in his hands and put my finger where the nails were, and put my hand into His side, I will not believe it" (John 20:25). Thomas and the queen of Sheba believed because they saw with their own eyes. But Jesus says, "Blessed are those who have not seen and yet have believed" (John 20:29).

The earthly kingdom of Solomon did not last. His son reigned for only five years before it began to collapse, "In the fifth year of King Rehoboam, Shishak king of Egypt, attacked Jerusalem. He carried off the treasures of the temple of the Lord and the treasures of the royal palace" (1 Kings 14:25-26). But the wealth of the kingdom of heaven will last forever (Matt. 6:19-21).

We receive a portion of that wealth when, through faith in Christ, our sins are forgiven. We share that wealth when we forgive those who have sinned against us (Matt. 18:21-22). But the complete glory of God's kingdom will not be revealed until the last day. Then we will see heaven in all its glory, as St. John envisioned. "The foundations of the city walls were decorated with every kind of precious stone . . . jasper . . . emerald . . . topaz and . . . amethyst. The twelve gates were twelve pearls, each gate made of a single pearl. The great street of the city was of pure gold, like transparent glass" (Rev. 21:18-21). There, we will reign with Christ forever (2 Tim. 2:12).

Prayer: Lord Jesus, thank You for preparing a place for me in Your kingdom. I know You will reveal its glory when You return. Keep me faithful until then. Amen.

Nehemiah
Comforter

Readings: Nehemiah 2 and 2 Corinthians 1:3-7

The name Nehemiah means, "The Lord Comforts." Yet, there was little to comfort Nehemiah when the people he loved lived in a city with no walls. Now that their Babylonian captivity was over many of God's faithful people had moved back to Jerusalem. But they found it demolished. It was burned to the ground, and the outer walls of defense were completely destroyed. The people were frail and defenseless. They were at the complete mercy of any enemy that would come upon them. Knowing their dangerous situation, Nehemiah's heart went out to them. He even wept for them (Neh. 1:3-4).

Nehemiah was in a position of great authority. He was the official cupbearer to King Artaxerxes (Neh. 1:11). That meant he could talk to the king. He had the ear of the most powerful man in the world. What a tremendous position. It was a position of high honor he was willing to use, and then give up for the benefit of the ones he loved. He asked the king if he might go to Jerusalem and help his people rebuild the city (Neh. 2:5).

With the king's permission, Nehemiah went to Jerusalem and began a great reconstruction project (Neh. 2:17-18). But all did not go well. His enemies conspired against him (Neh. 4:7-11). Yet, their efforts were in vain. Nehemiah succeeded in rebuilding the wall, and his enemies lost their confidence and became afraid because they realized the work was done with the help of God (Neh. 6:15-16). Now Nehemiah's people were protected.

This is a beautiful picture of what our Lord Jesus has done for us to give us His divine comfort and protection. Jesus was also in a position of great authority. Being one with the Father, all the majesty of heaven was His. Yet He gave up all the glory and set it aside to come to earth for our benefit (Phil. 2:6-7). He lived and worked like Nehemiah, so that we could have comfort and protection from our enemies. As St. Paul explains, "Praise be to the God and Father of our Lord Jesus Christ, the Father of compassion and the God of all comfort, who comforts us in all our troubles, so that we can comfort those in any trouble with the comfort we ourselves have received from God. For just as the sufferings of Christ flow over into our lives, so also through Christ our comfort overflows" (2 Cor 1:3-5).

Even though, like Nehemiah, Jesus' enemies conspired against him (Matt. 26:4, Mark 3:6), our Lord was successful. The love He showed us on the cross comforts us in time of sorrow, grief, or regret. When the enemies of chaos and confusion attack us, we have the comfort of His peace.

When sin and guilt assault us, we have the comfort of His forgiveness. When evil surrounds us, we have the comfort of His goodness and mercy. Let such enemies cower in fear; in Christ we have the protection and comfort of the Lord.

Prayer: Lord, as the psalmist wrote long ago, "My comfort in my suffering is this: Your promise preserves my life" (Ps. 119:50). Thank You Lord for keeping all Your promises in Jesus. Amen.

David (2)
Good Shepherd

Readings: Psalm 23 and John 10: 11-18

We can learn much concerning the trials and troubles of the shepherds of the Old Testament by reading their own descriptions of their work. Jacob worked for his Uncle Laban as a shepherd for 20 years. Jacob describes his work with these words, "This was my situation: The heat consumed me in the daytime and the cold at night, and sleep fled from my eyes" (Gen. 31:40).

David described his shepherding experience to King Saul saying, "Your servant has been keeping his father's sheep. When a lion or a bear came and carried off a sheep from the flock, I went after it, struck it and rescued the sheep from its mouth. When it turned on me, I seized it by its hair, struck it and killed it. Your servant has killed both the lion and the bear" (1 Sam. 17:34-36). There was nothing glamorous about being a shepherd. It was difficult and dangerous. It was not for the faint of heart. Not just anyone could be a good shepherd.

As sheep in the Lord's flock, we know what it is like to be attacked. Peter tells us, "Your enemy the devil prowls around like a roaring lion looking for someone to devour" (1 Pet. 5:8). But our Good Shepherd, Jesus Christ—like David, who fought both lion and bear—has fought this lion for us. Satan can no longer harm us—as Luther writes, "This world's prince may still Scowl fierce as he will, He can harm us none, He's judged; the deed is done; One little word can fell him" (*A Mighty Fortress*, stanza 3).

What other beasts are attacking you? Perhaps you are wrestling with a prolonged illness that has attacked you or a loved one. Maybe you are wrestling with guilt from a past sin that continues to haunt your conscience. You might be wrestling with a reoccurring temptation that will not leave you alone. Remember, Jesus is your Good Shepherd. No matter what struggles you have, Jesus is with you to protect and defend you from all evil (Ps 32:7). If you have strayed from his side, Jesus will find you (Ezek. 34:11-24; Matt. 18:12-14).

At one time our Good Shepherd was struck down, and the sheep temporarily scattered (Zech. 13:7; Mark 14:27, 46-50). Now, "He gathers the lambs in His arms and carries them close to His heart; He gently leads those that have young" (Is. 40:11). In times of confusion and uncertainty, He leads you with his Word. In times of grief and mourning, He comforts you with His tender love. In times of sin and failure, He restores your soul with His forgiveness. In times of chaos and despair, He consoles you in the still waters of your Baptism.

In times of conflict, when your enemies attack you, He prepares a table for you and feeds you with His own precious supper. Every day we live in the shadow of death but we need not fear. Jesus, the Good Shepherd is with us. He will guide us all of our lives. Then, at the time of His choosing, He will lead us to our eternal home.

Prayer: Lord Jesus, You have made me Your little lamb. In my Baptism, You have called me by name and added me to Your flock. Help me to always trust in You and look to You to satisfy my every need. Amen

Balm of Gilead
Divine Cure

Readings: Jeremiah 8:22 and Mark 2:1-12

Most of us know what it is like to be sick. The last time I had the flu I had a pounding headache, fever, and I was sick to my stomach. As uncomfortable as I was, that was nothing compared to others who suffer from much more serious ailments, such as cancer or heart disease.

God, in His mercy, has greatly blessed us with modern medicine, advanced technology, and many dedicated health care professionals. Through their work and the cures they distribute, He often touches us with His healing hands.

During the days of ancient Israel, God also used medicine to heal His people. One medicine that was especially popular was balm from Gilead. It must have had strong curative properties. It was not only used throughout Israel, but it was also shipped to places as far away as Egypt (Gen. 37:25) and Phoenicia (Ezek. 27:17).

No one knows exactly what this balm was. It must have been a salve or ointment made from the sap of a tree commonly found in Gilead. But whatever it was, it was a beneficial medicine that God used to heal many people. But where can we go to find healing for our souls? We can search the world over but there is no earthly cure for spiritual ills (Lam. 2:13). So Jeremiah could write, "Is there no balm in Gilead? Is there no physician there? Why then is there no healing for the wound of my people?" (Jer. 8:22). There was no healing for their spiritual afflictions because they were looking in the wrong place. They trusted in themselves—in their own accomplishments—their own alliances—their own strength. They were using the wrong medicine. They needed the healing that only God could give.

Beginning with a tone of sarcasm, Jeremiah told the Egyptians the same thing, "Go up to Gilead and get balm, O Virgin Daughter of Egypt. But you multiply your remedies in vain; there is no healing for you" (Jer. 46:11). In other words, go ahead and look as far as Gilead—search the world over if you like. But it will do you no good. There is no healing for a sin-sick soul apart from God.

The Lord makes it clear that He Himself will be our physician. "I will restore you to health and heal your wounds" (Jer. 30:17). He does that only through Jesus. Only Jesus can heal a conscience wounded by guilt. Only Jesus can cure a soul that is bruised and bloodied by the self-inflicted wounds of pride and arrogance. Only Jesus can restore your spiritual health, as well as your physical health (Mark 2:1-12).

This spiritual healing he has for you is not from the sap of the trees in Gilead, but from the blood of the cross on Calvary. "By His wounds you have been healed" (1 Pet. 2:24). All who know Christ can confess with Jeremiah, "Heal me, O Lord, and I will be healed; save me and I will be saved, for you are the one I praise" (Jer. 17:14).

Prayer: Dear Jesus, You are the cure and You are the physician. I look to You to heal my body and my soul. Please sooth my guilty conscience with the balm of your forgiveness. Amen.

Hosea
Faithful Husband

Readings: Hosea 3:1-2 and Ephesians 5:29-32

The prophet Hosea married Gomer—a woman who did not have the best reputation (Hos. 1:2-3). After a time Gomer proved to be unfaithful. Her situation went from bad to worse. She eventually ended up as a slave. Hosea had every right to turn his back on her but he did not.

With the Lord's encouragement Hosea remained a faithful husband. "The LORD said to me, 'Go, show your love to your wife again, though she is loved by another and is an adulteress. Love her as the LORD loves the Israelites, though they turn to other gods . . . ' So I bought her for fifteen shekels of silver and about a homer and a lethek [10 bushels] of barley" (Hos. 3:1-2).

Gomer had done nothing to earn her husband's kindness. Quite to the contrary, she did everything to earn his wrath. But Hosea (whose name means "salvation") loved her consistently and saved her from a life of slavery.

Here we have a beautiful example of the great underserved love Jesus has for each one of us. Note the amount Hosea paid for Gomer, "fifteen shekels of silver and about a homer and a lethek [10 bushels] of barley." All together the payment totaled 30 shekels—just as Jesus was sold for 30 pieces of silver (Matt. 26:14-16). Thirty shekels of silver was the cost of a slave in ancient Israel (Ex. 21:32). Jesus was sold as a slave to free us from the slavery of sin. Such was His great love for us in spite of our unfaithfulness.

Like Gomer, in her relationship with Hosea, we too have been unfaithful in our relationship with the Lord. We have sinned against God and, like Gomer, we too deserve nothing but wrath. But God treats us just like Hosea treated his wife. Instead of rejecting us, He comes to us—in Jesus—with salvation. Jesus loves you with an endless love. You may even turn your back on Him and forsake Him, like Gomer did to Hosea. But Jesus will never stop loving you—just as the waiting father never stopped loving the prodigal son (Luke 15:11-32).

He loves you as much as a groom loves his bride. Solomon expresses that intense love in his special love song when he writes, "You have stolen my heart, . . . you have stolen my heart with one glance of your eyes, with one jewel of your necklace. How delightful is your love . . . . How much more pleasing is your love than wine, and the fragrance of your perfume than any spice!" (Song of Sol. 4:9-10). That's how much Jesus loves you. You are indeed precious in His sight.

Just as the bond of love unite a husband and wife (Eph. 5:31), so also, the bond of love unites you with Christ. For Christ says to you, "I will betroth you to Me forever; I will betroth you in righteousness and justice, in love and compassion. I will betroth you in faithfulness" (Hos. 2:19-20). You are His, now and always (Rev. 19:7-8).

Prayer: Lord Jesus, I thank You for Your great love. Even though I am undeserving and at times I have forsaken You, You have never forsaken me. In the midst of this everchanging and confusing world, I know I can always count on Your love. Amen.

Amos
Burden Bearer

Readings: Amos 7:10-13 and 1 Peter 2:24

Amos was a shepherd (Amos 7:14). Yet, God gave Amos (whose name means "burden bearer") a very heavy load to carry. Although he was from Judah, God told him to go to Israel, point out their evil ways and warn them of their coming destruction. No one likes to be criticized. No one likes to hear bad news. Too many people want to shoot the messenger. As he preached to the people, Amos was viewed as an outsider who was sticking his nose into business where it did not belong. The people did not like him. They did not appreciate his message. They told him to go back home (Amos 7:12).

God loved the people of Israel, but He would not tolerate their evil ways. He had blessed their country with great prosperity. They were living an indulgent lifestyle and basking in the lap of luxury. Yet, they oppressed the poor (Amos 5:12). Their merchants fixed prices and cheated their customers (Amos 8:5). Their worship was empty and insincere (Amos 5:21-24). God was not going to put up with it anymore (Amos 8:1-2). They had ignored God's previous warnings (Amos 4:7-11). Now Amos had the burden of telling them of God's approaching destruction (Amos 7:17).

Like Amos, Jesus was also a shepherd (John 10:11). Jesus also came a great distance, from heaven to earth (John 6:38; 8:14). He also carried a great burden. Like Amos, Jesus had the burden of showing people their sins (Matt.

23:13-36). He too was rejected (Mark 8:31, Luke 4:24-30).

Yet, Jesus carried an even greater burden. He carried the sins of the world. Concerning Jesus, Isaiah prophesied, "He bore the sin of many" (Is. 53:12). St. Peter also wrote of Jesus, "He Himself bore our sins in His body on the tree" (1 Pet. 2:24). Jesus carried the burden of our sins to the cross. We don't have to carry the burden of guilt for the sins in our past. We don't have to carry the burden of fear concerning the possible sins of our future. Jesus has taken away all our sins—along with all their guilt and fear.

If Jesus loves us so much that He was willing to take the burden of our sins to Calvary, we can rest assured that He will be with us to carry our other burdens as well (Rom. 8:32, 1 Pet. 5:7). Jesus not only died for you, but since the first Easter, He also lives for you—to be with you to uphold you, to support you and yes, even to carry you through difficult times.

What is burdening you today? What trials are pressing on your mind? What concerns give you a heavy heart? Give them all over to Jesus and He will carry them for you. He calls out to you today, "Come to me, all you who are weary and burdened, and I will give you rest" (Matt. 11:28). Jesus is our "Amos"—our burden-bearer. "Praise be to the Lord, to God our Savior, who daily bears our burdens" (Ps 68:19).

Prayer: Dear Jesus, my burdens are so great. I cannot carry them alone. Today I hand them all over to You. Take away the all the sins and the fears that press so heavily against my heart. Amen.

Obadiah
Servant of the Lord

Readings: Obadiah 1-2 and Philippians 2:5-8

The name Obadiah means "Servant of the Lord."
Obadiah served the Lord in a very special way. In one
little book (Obadiah is the shortest book in the Old
Testament.), he proclaims a powerful message that warns
some of God's wrath; yet, also comforts others with His
grace.

He does it all by telling them about the Day of the Lord.
This is the Day of Judgment, which is coming for Edom
(Obad. 8) and for all the nations (Obad. 15). On that day
the enemies of the Lord will experience His wrath and
punishment. But His faithful children will find their
fulfillment and vindication. Warning God's enemies and
comforting God's people made Obadiah a valuable
servant indeed.

Isaiah tells us of a greater servant to come—Jesus. "See,
my servant will act wisely; He will be raised and lifted up
and highly exalted . . . But He was pierced for our
transgressions, He was crushed for our iniquities; the
punishment that brought us peace was upon Him, and by
His wounds we are healed" (Is. 52:13; 53:5).

Like Obadiah before Him, Jesus would have a twofold
task. He would conquer God's enemies while also
comforting and vindicating God's people. This too would
take place on one special day—Good Friday. This could
only happen by Jesus becoming a suffering servant.

Jesus was flogged, stripped of His clothes, spit upon, and ridiculed. He was given a crown of thorns and then crucified (Matt. 27:26-31). Jesus willingly endured unspeakable torment because of His great love for us.

St. Paul explains the wonder of it all when he writes, that Jesus, "Who, being in very nature God, did not consider equality with God something to be grasped, but made Himself nothing, taking the very nature of a servant, being made in human likeness. And being found in appearance as a man, He humbled Himself and became obedient to death—even death on a cross!" (Phil. 2:6-8).

Then, after three days, He who was raised up on the cross to die in shame was raised up to life to manifest His glory. Then, "God exalted Him to the highest place and gave Him the name that is above every name, that at the name of Jesus every knee should bow, in heaven and on earth and under the earth, and every tongue confess that Jesus Christ is Lord, to the glory of God the Father" (Phil. 2:9-11).

Jesus' entire ministry from beginning to end was one of service, "This was to fulfill what was spoken through the prophet Isaiah: 'Here is my servant whom I have chosen'" (Matt. 12:17-18). Like Obadiah before Him, Jesus was a true servant of the Lord.

Prayer: Dear Jesus, how can I ever repay You for all that You have done for me? Send your Holy Spirit into my heart and enable me to show my gratitude for Your service, by being a servant for others. Amen.

Jonah
Buried for Three Days

Readings: Jonah 1:1-17 and Matthew 12:38-41

The Lord told Jonah to go preach His word to the people of Nineveh, to the east. But instead, Jonah gets on a boat to Tarshish and heads west. But try as he might there was no way to avoid the Lord's mission. The judgment of God fell upon Jonah so that a violent storm arose and nearly sank the ship. Jonah knew he could not escape. He willingly accepted God's verdict.

So to quiet the sea and save the sailors, Jonah told them, "Pick me up and throw me into the sea . . . and it will become calm. I know that it is my fault that this great storm has come upon you" (Jon. 1:12). This early in the story we already see a picture of Jesus. Unlike Jonah, Jesus had done no wrong; nevertheless, Jesus accepted the guilty verdict of His Father for us. He knew He must die. As Jesus hung on Calvary's cross, the wrath of God swamped over Him and consumed Him (Ps. 88, especially verses 7 and 16).

The Lord caused a huge fish to swallow up Jonah, and he remained inside the stomach of the fish for three days and three nights (Jon. 1:17). So also when Jesus died, He was placed inside the tomb for three days. Jesus Himself made this comparison, "For as Jonah was three days and three nights in the belly of a huge fish, so the Son of Man will be three days and three nights in the heart of the earth" (Matt. 12:40). After three days the huge fish vomited Jonah onto the land (Jon. 2:10). The fish released Jonah at God's command.

So also after three days, death could not hold our crucified Lord (Acts 2:24). He gloriously rose from the dead just as He said He would (Luke 24:1-8). After being released on the ground, Jonah went to Nineveh and proclaimed God's Word. The king repented. The Ninevites believed and many were saved (Jon. 3:3, 10). So also after our Lord's resurrection, the preaching of his Word goes forth today and many are saved. Just as Jonah preached to the Ninevites, so Jesus still is sending His Holy Spirit into the hearts of pastors, teachers, parents, and to all who share His Good News of salvation. Jesus explained to His disciples, "This is what is written: The Christ will suffer and rise from the dead on the third day, and repentance and forgiveness of sins will be preached in His name to all nations, beginning at Jerusalem" (Luke 24:46-47).

We can learn a great deal from Jonah. Let's not turn and run from those who need to hear God's Word. May our Lord's resurrection inspire us to share the message of His love at appropriate times and in winsome ways (1 Pet. 3:15). Some people are unwilling to follow the example of the Ninevites. They believed and were saved. Some today refuse to listen to the words of Jesus even though He is raised from the dead (Luke 16:27-31). These doubters and skeptics need our love, our persistence, our patience, and our prayers.

Prayer: Lord Jesus, just as Jonah was inside the great fish, so also for three days You were in the grave. Help me to share the message of Your glorious resurrection. Send your Spirit to open the hearts of those who do not yet believe. Amen.

Zerubbabel
Carpenter

Readings: Zechariah 4:6-14 and Matthew 16:18

In 538 B.C., 70 years of Babylonian captivity came to an end for God's people. Zerubbabel and Jeshua led the first group of exiles back to Jerusalem (Ezra 2:1-2). One of the first items of business was to rebuild the Lord's temple (Ezra 3:8-9). The prophets Haggai (Hag. 1:3, 13-14) and Zechariah (Zech. 4:6-14) gave them a great deal of encouragement.

Even though there was opposition (Ezra 4:1-5), God blessed the efforts of Zerubbabel the governor, and Jeshua the high priest. Their work was successful and the new temple was completed in three and a half years (Ezra 6:13-15). Both Zerubbabel and Jeshua (whose name also can be translated "Jesus"), point our attention to our Lord Jesus, who directs an even bigger construction project.

Jesus' earthly stepfather was a carpenter (Matt. 13:55). Jesus Himself was known by that same trade (Mark 6:3). No doubt Joseph taught Jesus his skills of woodworking. As a carpenter, Jesus knew what it was like to be involved in a construction project. In Nazareth where Jesus grew up, there were no buildings as large as the Jerusalem temple. But Jesus is in charge of building something much larger—His church.

When Peter confessed that Jesus was the Christ, the Son of the living God (Matt. 16:16), Jesus replied, "On this rock I will build My church" (Matt. 16:18). The church that Jesus builds is not made of wood or stone, but people—not just any people—but those who confess Him as their Lord and Savior. Jesus himself is the cornerstone (Ps. 118:22, Is. 28:16), and the prophets and apostles are the foundation (Eph. 2:19-22).

Just as a skilled carpenter uses a hammer or a saw, (or as Zerubbabel used a plumb line, Zech. 4:10), so also Jesus uses His special tools—His Word and sacraments. By the power of His Word, He created the universe (Ps. 33:6, 9, Heb. 11:3). So also by the power of His Word, He calls us out of darkness and into the light of His kingdom of grace—His holy Christian church.

Jesus builds His church one person at a time as each new believer comes to have faith in Him as His Lord and Savior. It is only in His church that you have the beginning of the joy and peace that will be yours in abundance in heaven.

By God's grace, His church is expanding to include people across the globe from every tribe and race (Matt. 13:31-32, Rev. 7:9). The fiercest opposition cannot defeat it. Even the gates of hell will not stand up against it (Matt. 16:18).

As we assist the Lord in His building project, let us build each other up (1 Thess. 5:11, Jude 20) and strengthen each other in our Christian faith that we might remain in His kingdom now and forever.

Prayer: Thank you Lord for calling me into Your church. It gives me a great sense of comfort and belonging. May Your powerful Word be proclaimed throughout the world so that Your kingdom of grace may come to everyone. Amen.

A Purifying Fountain
Washes Us Clean

Readings: Zechariah 13:1 and Revelation 7:13-14

When God gave the children of Israel the instructions for building the tabernacle, He told them also to build a large basin or caldron in which to keep water for ceremonial washing. The priests were to wash their hands to prepare to touch holy things. They were also to wash their feet to prepare to walk on holy ground. Only after they washed could they then enter the tabernacle or offer burnt sacrifices to the Lord. Failure to properly wash would bring certain death (Ex. 30:17-21).

Much later when King Solomon built a more elaborate temple, the water basin was replaced by a huge bowl-shaped reservoir of water called The Sea, which held about 17,500 gallons. This too was used specifically for the washing of the priests (2 Chron. 4:4- 6).

These ceremonial washings not only made the priests ritually clean to offer the burnt sacrifices, but they also pointed toward a greater cleansing—this is the one Ezekiel spoke of when he wrote, "I will sprinkle clean water on you, and you will be clean; I will cleanse you from all your impurities and from all your idols. . . . I will save you from all your uncleanness" (Ezek. 36:25, 29).

This is the same one Zechariah speaks of when he says, "On that day a fountain will be opened to the house of David and the inhabitants of Jerusalem, to cleanse them from sin and impurity" (Zech. 13:1).

That fountain is our Lord Jesus Christ. He is the only one who can wash us clean from the filthy stain of our sins. Jesus demonstrated that when, "A man with leprosy came and knelt before Him and said, 'Lord, if You are willing, You can make me clean.' Jesus reached out His hand and touched the man. 'I am willing,' He said. 'Be clean!' Immediately he was cured of his leprosy" (Matt. 8:2-3). Jesus cleaned the man of his leprosy to show him and us that He can cleanse us from our greatest filth— even our sin.

One way the Lord cleanses us of our sins is through the waters of our Baptism. Ananias said to Paul, "Get up and be baptized and wash your sins away, calling on His name" (Acts 22:16). So also Paul would later write, "He saved us, not because of righteous things we had done, but because of His mercy. He saved us through the washing of rebirth and renewal by the Holy Spirit, whom He poured out on us generously through Jesus Christ our Savior" (Titus 3:5-6).

Like the ancient priests of Israel, being properly cleaned is a matter of life and death. If we do not have our sins washed away by the fountain of Christ, we face eternal death (John 3:36). But being cleansed of our sins and clothed in His righteousness we have everlasting life (Rev. 7:13-14).

Prayer: "Nothing in my hand I bring; Simply to thy cross I cling. Naked, come to thee for dress; Helpless look to thee for grace; Foul I to the fountain fly; Wash me Savior or I die." Amen. *(Rock of Ages, stanza 3)*

Malachi
God's Messenger

Readings: Malachi 1:1 and John 1:14

I still remember quite vividly a seminary professor I had who would frequently shout to his students, "Speak up!" He must have been hard of hearing. Questions always were encouraged and his answers sharp and insightful, but he had very little patience with inquiries posed by timid, soft-spoken seminarians, sitting in the back row of the classroom. God has made us humans to be the crown of creation (Gen. 1:26-27, Ps. 8:6-8). We are indeed fearfully and wonderfully made (Ps. 139:14). But no one I know and trust has been given the ability to read minds. If we want people to know what we are thinking, we have to speak up.

That is exactly what God has done throughout history. He wants us to know what He is thinking and He has spoken. He has done this in many ways. He has spoken through angels (e.g., Luke 1:11 -19, the word "angel" means "messenger"), dreams (e.g., Gen. 20:3-6), visions (e.g., Gen. 15:1), prophets (e.g., Judg. 6:7-10), and apostles (e.g., Luke 9:1-2). The name Malachi means "my messenger". He received a message from God, and it was his task to present that message to God's people (Mal. 1:1) just as John the Baptizer did many years later (Mal. 3:1).

All of these visions, dreams, and messengers, point to a greater messenger who was yet to come. Moses wrote, "The LORD your God will raise up for you a prophet like me from among your own brothers. You must listen to Him. . . . I will raise up for them a prophet like you from among their brothers; I will put My words in his mouth, and He will tell them everything I command Him. If anyone does not listen to My words that the prophet speaks in My name, I Myself will call him to account" (Deut. 18:15-19). So also the author of the letter to the Hebrews writes, "In the past God spoke to our forefathers through the prophets at many times and in various ways, but in these last days He has spoken to us by His Son" (Heb. 1:1-2).

Today God speaks to us through His Word made flesh, Jesus Christ. Just as your words reveal your thoughts, so Jesus, in His preaching and teaching and dying, reveals the thoughts of God (John 1:14). Concerning His teaching, Jesus could say, "These words you hear are not My own; they belong to the Father who sent Me" (John 14:24). God wants us to hear what He has to say through Jesus. At the transfiguration of Jesus the voice of the heavenly Father said, "This is My Son, whom I love. Listen to Him!" (Mark 9:7).

Through His final and most important of all messengers—Jesus Christ, God speaks to you His message of sincere love. His love for you is great (John 15:13). His love for you is everlasting (Rom. 8:35-39). No one needs to tell God to "Speak up!" He has spoken loudly and clearly in His Son Jesus Christ—to tell you that He loves you now and forever.

Prayer: Heavenly Father, I thank You for the tremendous love You have given me through Christ Jesus—the greatest of all Your messengers. Help me to trust in that love always. Embolden me to love others as You have loved me. Amen.

Refiner's Fire
Destroys All Evil

Readings: Malachi 3:2-3 and Luke 3:17

When you read the newspapers or watch the evening news, you can't help but notice the terrible and vicious evil that occasionally manifests itself—senseless acts of hatred against racial minorities— horrific acts of violence against innocent children— Christians who are tortured because of the faith—women who are repeatedly abused and subject to unspeakable degradation—if you dwell on such thoughts long enough (sometimes not long at all), it can bring you to tears. The power and the scope of evil can be over- whelming. There seems to be no end in sight.

Throughout the ages God's faithful people have pleaded to heaven, "O LORD, the God who avenges, O God who avenges, shine forth. Rise up, O Judge of the earth; pay back to the proud what they deserve. How long will the wicked, O LORD, how long will the wicked be jubilant? They pour out arrogant words; all the evildoers are full of boasting. They crush your people, O LORD; they oppress your inheritance. They slay the widow and the alien; they murder the fatherless. They say, "The LORD does not see; the God of Jacob pays no heed" (Ps. 94:1-7; see also Ps. 10 and Hab.1:2-4).

Where is God? Has He deserted us (Ezek. 9:9)? Is He unaware of what is going on (Ps. 94: 9)? Is He asleep (Ps. 44:23)? The Good News is that God hears the cries of his people (Ex. 2:23-25, Ps. 34:17-18). He is fully aware of the wickedness in this world, and He has sent His Son to destroy all evil. Malachi looked forward to that day when he wrote, "'Surely the day is coming; it will burn like a furnace. All the arrogant and every evildoer will be stubble, and that day that is coming will set them on fire,' says the LORD Almighty. 'Not a root or a branch will be left to them. But for you who revere My name, the sun of righteousness will rise with healing in its wings. And you will go out and leap like calves released from the stall. Then you will trample down the wicked; they will be ashes under the soles of your feet on the day when I do these things,' says the LORD Almighty" (Mal. 4:1-3).

That day is the end of the world. But it already has begun to come through Christ—right now! Through His suffering and death on the cross, Christ has conquered the forces of evil. A new age of love and forgiveness has begun in Christ. This new reign of Christ is powerfully manifest in the hearts and lives of all who believe in Jesus.

But this is just the beginning. The day is coming when Jesus will return, and we will see the fulfillment of our salvation. His reign will be clear and visible over all creation. At that time, all evil, hatred, and cruelty will be destroyed. Right will triumph over wrong. Good will be victorious over evil. There will be no more pain, hunger, or suffering. This is the day for which all creation longs (Rom. 8:22).

Prayer: Lord, it is not easy being patient. Help me to trust in Your timing. Never let me doubt Your power or Your love. Strengthen me so that with Your might I stand firm against the evil in this world. Come quickly Lord Jesus. Amen

Topic Index

Scripture Index

Below are listed all the Bible passages used in the preceding forty devotions. The eighty main readings are listed in **bold** print

Proverbs

Song of Solomon

Isaiah

Jeremiah

88

90